MASTER GIFTS

Permission to live without fear and on purpose

KAREN WEAVER

National Library of Australia Cataloguing-in-Publication data:
The Alchemy og Life/Making Magic Happen Academy
Romance – fiction

ISBN:

Each day brings new magic.

CONTENTS

INTRODUCTION

The Alchemy of Life Magic Mastery is all about living on purpose and without fear. I have journeyed with these seven master gifts for the past seven years. I wrote and published 'Mindful Magic' back in 2017, and this book series has my heart and is my life's legacy. I have grown so much throughout these seven years. The insights, the pearls of wisdom, everything that's been channeled, is all for you to embrace.

I hope that you find some gold in here. I hope that these master gifts enhance your life and serve as a stepping stone on your path to awakening your full potential. I am called to share with you, the readers, a bridge to awakening, where you can then explore further. Over the years, I have read many books on the subjects of universal laws, awakening, philosophies, and principles—so many.

But I have also been intuitively guided to share my knowledge and experiences in a digestible form, so that I'm communicating with you and sharing my experiences, thoughts, and musings with you. My intention is to help you benefit from and embrace what resonates with you. I'm not here to dictate or preach. I am simply sharing in the hope that my experiences and thoughts will enrich your life and expand it beyond your wildest imagination. Dreams do come true, but first, you need to embrace them, believe in them, get to know who you are, and embark on the journey.

There will be a bumpy ride. Before every breakthrough, there's a struggle. The extent of the struggle will depend on how much work you have to do to make your dreams the very next step. But I promise you one thing: if you do the work, you will be rewarded. So think of me as your big sister, holding your hand, and sharing my experiences with you, because believe me, it's been messy.

But I never regret one moment of my life. There has been so much joy, so much success, so much wisdom, so much good. And I always choose the positive over the negative. So I will continue to focus on the good things in my life and learn from the not-so-good, because that's what it's all about. We should always be advancing.

We never stop advancing, no matter how high we go.

So I raise this cup to you in the hope that this book serves you well, and I would love to hear from you. Come and join me in my Facebook group, 'Light Magic Mastery with KP Weaver.' And I hope that these seven master gifts are a breakthrough for you.

The Magic
of Mindfulness

*Mindfulness is not about changing
who you are, it's about enhancing the
experience of being you.*

EARLY MINDSET EXPERIENCES

I was blessed with a childhood where I felt safe to explore life and its potential. Even though I grew up in Northern Ireland during the time of the troubles, when soldiers walked around with guns and bomb scares were daily occurrences, my parents' mindset was of acknowledging the fear but choosing to allow us a non-fear-based platform to grow from. I remember feeling loved unconditionally and that type of love gives you a super powerful mindset – Superpower.

You may not have the power to control where you begin your life, but you do have the power to choose where you live it.

Briefly use the space below to share your childhood feeling experience. (Hugs to anyone who needs one right now).

'The difference between how magical life felt when you were a child and how your life might be now is because you stopped believing in the magic of life.'
Rhonda Byrne

MINDSET AND FEAR

Often parents (and I am one of the guilty ones) instill fears in their children to protect them from the potential dangers they may face in life. If my child has not listened to my reasonable explanation about why they should not run off then I will talk about the 'Boogy Man'. I never thought I would ever share such tales and in fact I was very much against it until I had girls! But it is amazing the personal boundaries you will surpass with each child you have. My girls are more adventurous and push the boundaries way further than my boys ever did. With six children you have to instill something to make them think twice and the Boogy Man worked so the Boogy Man it is.

Something that fascinated me about the extent to which a mother would go to lovingly protect her daughters was the discovery of the reason behind the lack of a mother figure in fairytales. It is because it was often the mothers who made up the stories to help their daughters become more resilient should they ever be taken away or lose their life. Growing up in Ireland meant I was very familiar with traditional fairytales.

A beautiful story comes to mind about my late dear friend Geraldine. I worked in a factory in my late teens to mid-twenties and one of my good friends in there was a real storyteller, I could listen to her forever. One day she told us the true story of how she and her sister made everyone believe they had real fairies at the bottom of the garden. They were so convincing that they made the front page of a 1970s Irish national newspaper at the time. She knew how to tell a story. One about a beautiful red-haired girl had the hair on the back of my neck standing on end when I was driving the Irish backroads from Crom Castle twenty years later!

It is when I am gifted with a deeper insight that I sit up and think differently. I love challenging my thought patterns and understand that most things have a deeper meaning that gifts us a greater understanding than what is perceived at face value. Everyone can benefit from being mindful of their rigid thought patterns for flexibility gifts freedom.

Fear can be limiting and as a mum, I can see why these stories were created. These fears are instilled with loving intention but they can limit our potential. Freedom of the mind can be deemed reckless but I would like to challenge that mindset by suggesting it is reckless of us to waste our lives conforming to the limitations of fear. How can we discover our magic when we reside in our comfort zone with walls of fear surrounding us?

Feel the fear and do it anyway.

Elizabeth Gilbert often talks about fear and her book *Big Magic* explores creative living beyond fear.

'Yes you absolutely do need your fear, in order to protect you from actual dangers…But you do not need your fear in the realm of creative expression.'
Elizabeth Gilbert

I went to listen to her at the Perth International Arts Festival in 2015. It felt strange for me to leave my young family to go out in the city on my own but I felt compelled to do so. I had touched base with Elizabeth on her Facebook page and she responded graciously that she would see me there. Of course I had hoped for a shout out but that didn't happen. Coincidentally there was a microphone set up at the stage beside my seat and yes, I shamelessly stated my seat number in the Facebook comment! But when she invited people to come forward to ask questions I refrained from the opportunity and didn't know why, because usually I would have been onto that straight away. Then the reason found me. After the event was over I was leaving via a side entrance and in a serendipitous moment I met her there. We exchanged a few words but it was her energy I connected with. I felt a familiar frequency from her to the one I had within myself, one comprised of magic. I instantly knew why I didn't get up during the event. This was to be our connection; it wasn't verbal, it was energy and I found the courage to open my shielded heart and brave the world again in that moment.

When time and circumstance align, magic happens.

Afterwards, empowered by the inspired interaction with Elizabeth Gilbert, I opened up my peripheral power and began to take action fully connected to the faith in my *Knowing*.

We all have the navigation tool required to discover our destiny. It is the most valuable tool in the universe and yet it costs nothing. There are those who think too much about how to find it, whereas it is the special knowing feeling that helps us to open up our heart core and allow the light to shine into our lives. I have been accessing it for years and I am blessed with the instant ability to connect.

> **'Sometimes we have to ponder life to discover**
> **the answers we are searching for.'**
> *Bella Blue*

Many people pay for mentors to help them find their answers when some stillness can gift us clarity. Follow that with some mindfulness and it can be enough to change anyone's life.

A little about my journey inward

Have you ever heard the saying *Go within or go without*? I wrote an article about it when I was evolving and it is included in my book *Heart Writer* and also in the back of this book.

I went through a pretty rough time during the second half of 2006 and all of 2007. I suffered Post Traumatic Stress Disorder (PTSD) and it totally altered my perspective on life. I became an introvert and this was totally the opposite of who I was. It is such a cliché but I was as low as I could possibly go and from there the only way was up.

So when more than a year later I endured something that shook me to my core I didn't know if I could handle the heartache. Losing my twin pregnancy was the most painful thing I have ever endured in my life. The pain of that loss was a physical pain, one that I will never forget. It pierced through my every thought, my heart was broken but it woke me up. I could feel again! I cried rivers of tears, for the babies I would never hold and for the year and a half of my life that I could never get back. I began to realise things that I never fully understood before. It was as if the whole time I was focused within was not wasted after all, it was a time when I observed life. I became more aware of the smaller things in life, I felt more knowledgeable.

I liken this time of my life to the metamorphosis of a butterfly. I was once a colourful caterpillar consuming as much as I could before I went into a cocoon where I lay still going through the motions of life until the time when I could release myself from the darkness of the cocoon and begin to live again.

I realised it was not my fault I was put in that situation, it was beyond my control, but it was my choice how I chose to deal with it. At that time in my life I needed to go within and this incident guided me there but I had overstayed my time and so I had to wake up. This realisation empowered me, it clicked a switch and I had my power back. What had shaken me to my core was that I didn't feel safe, I didn't feel in control of my own life, and that's not a nice feeling at all for it takes away your liberty and self-worth.

Since then my life has been the way I would have only ever dreamt of before. We got pregnant the next month, we were granted a visa to go to Australia, we got married and we emigrated to the other side of the world.

THOUGHT AWARENESS

Being aware of your thoughts is the first major step towards creating a live you will love.

Our thoughts create our reality. They are responsible for the energy we emit. They are responsible for what we put out into the world and how others perceive us. They are all powerful. So it makes sense that we should be in control of them, right?

Mindfulness is the most natural way to control your thoughts. Being aware of what is happening around you is common sense! Then why do more of us not embrace it? Does it go against our human nature? Have we grown so far away from a mindful mindset that it takes a total conscious mind shift to help us find the perfect flow?

I am fascinated by how our minds work and especially how powerful they are. Our perceptions of life and the things that go on around us are often not aligned with where we want to be in life and so often you can feel unsettled, as if everything is against you or you just don't feel fulfilled.

If you can master your own thoughts and influence the thoughts of others, that's when you can make a REAL change.

I was intrigued by the psychology of *The Secret* when it swarmed the globe ten years ago. I read it in 2010, two years after moving to Australia. It was exactly what I needed to read at that moment in my life. I totally believe that when a book finds you at exactly the right time it shifts something within and your perspective on your world will not be the same again. This is a good thing when you are going against your flow, like I was. It was exactly what I needed to assist me in adjusting my perspective.

On paper I had the nice life. I was living the Irish dream of moving to Australia and at the time we had two boys and two girls but it seemed that every time I started to shine again something would drag me back. Why?

I couldn't see it then but I can clearly see now.

I wasn't living for me, I was living for others! I gave one hundred per cent to my family and didn't keep anything for myself. Anything I did try to salvage for myself was taken away by my hubby, who was highly stressed and didn't see why I should be happy if he was sacrificing all of himself for his family. I bore the weight of this for many years and sometimes I felt empathetic and the fixer in me wanted to help.

Then I discovered I was the one who had the power to change things. I didn't need to be a victim of circumstance. I had a right to be happy if that's what I chose to be, in fact ALL of my family would benefit from a happier me. My perspective began to shift and I began keeping some focus on me. I love being there for my family, it is one of my non-negotiables. I love being their carer, I love their hugs, I love their little noses and when they have grumpy faces. I love it when they shine and I love it when I have to nurse them back to health, I love all of this because I am a mum. But what kind of mother am I if I choose to sacrifice all of myself? I resolved that I would begin incrementally to pursue my dream. A dream that my childhood did not gift me the belief in achieving, but somehow the belief found me and ignited a strong passion inside me.

I now have the benefit of seeing in my children's eyes that they too know that if they want something, they can go get it! But they also value how hard you may need to work. I am happy to gift my children this. This is important to me. But it may not have been had I chosen to remain quiet, to play it safe. I chose to be brave and go forth to claim my dreams and you can too. You might not have to sacrifice as much as you think because others will see the passion burning inside you and make way for that magic to take hold.

Let everything you do be done in love.

This quote is the best piece of advice I can gift to anyone choosing to make magic happen in their lives. When I began studying The Law of Attraction I was beyond delighted to discover it was first called The Law of Love – a big 'Aha!' moment for me.

Take a moment to think about it. Look at the people making a difference in our world – Oprah, Mother Theresa, Elizabeth Gilbert, Louise Hay, Joanne Fedler, Peace Mitchell are a few on my list. These people have set aside any dependency on financial gain and opened their hearts to the world. They are brave yet they have pursued their heart-centred purpose with such intensity that we all feel the benefits and come to love them back, even though we may never have met them. We feel their energy directly. We trust them so we allow them into our hearts. Imagine a life where we could have our hearts open all of the time. Imagine how brave you need to be. Imagine how liberating it is.

I want you to think for one moment…what have you got to lose? I suggest you have nothing to lose and so much to gain.

It comes down to a feeling of *Knowing*. Once you set an intention it is your job to switch on your peripheral power and become good friends with the *Knowing* feeling. It is your guide! It will never let you down. Through this inbuilt personal navigation tool you will always stay on the right path that serves your greater good. We all have one, but quite often we don't know how to use it. I will be gifting my children the insight on how to use theirs – no batteries needed!

Knowing is not a thinking thing, it is a feeling thing – make it your best friend.

FIRST STEP ATTRACTION

Asking the Universe for something is the first step and it's the easy part– but the real thing you should be considering is if you are really ready to receive all that you are asking the Universe for. We are human after all and sometimes we can send signs to the Universe that we want something we are not physically, mentally or emotionally prepared to actively receive.

Asking for something is one thing, receiving it is another. I wrote about this subject in my second novel *The Wish Giver*. Five people were visited by the Wish Giver and each had sacrifices to make to allow them to receive their request. It was written on the principle that things shift around you to give you what you ask for and sometimes what you have to sacrifice isn't worth it.

To receive something, there has to be inspired action and conviction that you really want to receive. No matter what it is you want to manifest you must first consider what you may be sacrificing in the pursuit of your dream.

To receive money, you have to exert effort to receive it because that is simply how things work. The Law of Attraction never fails us – it gives us exactly what we want deep in our hearts.

So if you want something, you really have to break down your emotional and mental defences to allow your dreams to manifest in physical reality. You have to let the Universe know you are ready to receive it. You receive what you have the courage to believe.

'To accomplish great things we must not only act, but also dream; not only plan, but also believe.'
Anatole France

MINDFUL TASK

Before we begin I would like you to write a sentence in response to each of these questions.

What is mindfulness?

_____

What is magic?

_____

*Mindfulness is not about changing who you are,
it's about enhancing the experience of being you.
Don't compromise yourself in your pursuit of success.*

I can share with you the definitions of Mindfulness and Magic but I want you to define what they mean to you, right now in this very moment.

Before I continue I want to share with you why I wrote this book. I am passionate about the importance of what makes us pursue our dreams; our 'why' is a powerful essence in our journey.

One speech I connected with on a deep level was Matthew McConaghy's 2014 Oscar acceptance speech for Best Actor in *Dallas Buyers Club* when he spoke of three things he needed each day. I suggest you watch it as you will feel the emotion of its delivery. Words delivered through the heart channel reach down and nourish our soul, leaving a lasting impact, something to be mindful of.

> **'One, I need something to look up to, another is something to look forward to, and another is someone to chase.'**
> *Matthew McConaghy*

The speech has so much impact because he is truly living his calling in exactly the way he chooses to and without compromising the beliefs at the root of his being. He emphasises the need for us to follow our dreams but not to compromise too much of ourselves in the pursuit.

It really struck a chord with me because I am passionate about the same thing. I am always mindful that although I push boundaries I will always maintain a balance between my priorities of family, work and play. This is a key to maintaining a successful mindset and manifesting successfully in the long term.

I have learnt a lot about manifesting and tested it many times. I do however have some non-negotiables that I don't jeopardise in pursuit of my calling. One of my best pieces of advice to you is to connect with yourself wholeheartedly. Every action has a reaction. Once you open the doors to receiving, amazing things will come your way. That is why I fuse mindfulness with the magic of manifesting. When you have that balance right, you will have few regrets. You will maintain your personal essence, the fundamental characteristic that makes you wonderfully you. If you keep that close at heart you will never go wrong. It will call you back at times on the journey so be sure to listen and check back in, its intention is to protect your greater good. Aspire to be the best version of you.

Definition of Mindfulness

The quality or state of being conscious or aware of something.
Cambridge English Dictionary

Definition of Magic

*The use of special powers to make things happen
that would usually be impossible.*
Cambridge English Dictionary

INSTANT MINDSET SHIFTERS

Did you know that it takes three weeks to create a habit? You may read this fact a few times throughout this book but it is such an amazing piece of information to have instilled in your mind that I treat it as Gold.

There have been many occasions in my life when I have used this mindset to make dramatic changes. And somehow my mind allows me permission to make a dramatic change if it believes it only has to make the conscious effort for a few weeks. But of course after those three weeks of dedication your mind should have a new habit that feels more normal to execute.

I do this often when I am changing an eating habit. The first three weeks are so tough but after that, if I continue to make the right choices then it is much easier. It was the same when I gave up smoking. I loved it so much but for the greater good of my unborn baby I stopped and have never smoked again, but the first three weeks were the hardest. When I joined my first NaNoWriMo in 2010 it took three weeks to really find my flow of writing 1667 words every day but I did and that month I wrote a 50000 word novel, *The Visitor*. And believe me if I can make a life change in three weeks then so can you.

In those three weeks affirmations are really helpful. Below are some other possibilities.

- Affirmations
- Count to 10 before acting
- Three weeks of mindfulness
- Have a mindful reset button

- A mindset stone
- Mindful moments

Affirmations that are relevant to focusing your mindset on what you want to achieve can be very powerful. Whether it be money, happiness or health these little mind tricksters will make a real difference. Find affirmations that are relevant to what you want to achieve.

Counting to ten gives you time to think before you react. It's amazing how differently things can look ten seconds after you would have initially reacted. That space can gift the magic of clarity and avoid any regrettable actions that could arise.

The three weeks of mindfulness is a life-changing approach to instigating change or achieving goals.

Having a mindful reset button can reboot your mindset back to a more focused one clear of clutter.

I love having a mindset stone in my pocket or purse. I rub it and it has the power to instantly shift my energy. My stone of choice is a rose quartz, which is the love stone. You could look at different stones and see what resonates with you, because they all emit energy. Any stone will do though and when you have chosen your stone, sit with it and think of something that makes you feel good. Then when you touch the stone, feel that feeling and it will assist you in mindfully attracting magic into your life.

And finally, mindful moments. As we all have phones with us these days it is easy to have access to *mindful moments*. The way it works is to set your alarm with a nice tone to sound at different times throughout the day that work in with your schedule. When you hear the alarm you will feel good and that will reset your energy from what you have wound yourself into during that day. For the duration of the alarm going off, feel, feel, feel every magical tingle.

Mix and match these mindset shifters to work in with your life.

POWER OF THOUGHT

*If you want Magic to be a part of your life
you must first believe in Magic.*

Your thoughts are all powerful. They are energy and therefore instigate a reaction. Energy is what activates your energy field so be mindful of the thoughts that stream from your mind to your brain stem, instigating your nervous system to release a reaction out into your energy field.

Your energy field is strongest in close proximity.

Your energy field has the power to attract and deflect and is owned by your thoughts that are the creators of your feelings.

Every action causes a reaction.

The psychology behind the power of mindset can be difficult to comprehend with a closed mind, but when you open yourself up to possibilities anything can occur. My first experience of The Law of Attraction was through Rhonda Byrne's book *The Secret*. This book gifted me a deeper understanding of how powerful we all are. We are most definitely more than our body. The energy we create manifests our reality. I was intrigued by the knowledge and the 'Aha!' moments I had while reading this book. Everything made sense to me, it was as if my mind had opened wider than I could ever have imagined. I wanted to learn more, I needed to know more of this gold, it was totally aligned with how I wanted to think, totally aligned with what I knew to be.

'There is a truth deep down inside of you that has been waiting for you to discover it, and that truth is this: You deserve all good things life has to offer.'
Rhonda Byrne, The Secret

So too with Louise Hay's book, *You Can Heal Your Life*. The introduction to how powerful your mindset is in creating your health in a metaphysical sense is much less confronting than *The Secret* and yet just as powerful. This book also introduced me to the power of affirmations as an instant mind shift tool, enabling us to instantly connect with words that will trick our mind into initiating an emotion that is more aligned with our purpose, our health goals and ourselves.

There are no limits, only those we impose on ourselves.

We are all different and we all think differently! This is fabulous as can you imagine how bland the world would be if we were all the same? Variety is the spice of life! However, there is this universal law that is supported on a metaphysical level. What Louise Hay showed me is that I can shift my energy even if I am having a crap day or going through a rough time. I am in control of how to mindfully shift my energy and how I react. She taught me to be gentle with this new insight. She gifted me the power of affirmational knowledge. By saying something and feeling this power we can shift the power of our reality, thus shifting its outcome.

I recited this list of affirmations by Louise Hay every day when I was evolving. It helped me feel safe and trust that I was moving forward into my true self.

Deep at the centre of my being there is an infinite well of love.

I now allow this love to flow to the surface.

It fills my heart, my body, my mind, my consciousness, my very being, and radiates out from me in all directions and returns to me multiplied.

The more love I use and give, the more I have to give, the supply is endless.

The use of love makes me feel good; it is an expression of my inner joy.

Yes, I love myself, therefore I take loving care of my body.

I lovingly feed it nourishing food and beverages.

I lovingly groom it and dress it and my body lovingly responds to me with vibrant health and energy.

I love myself, therefore I provide for myself a comfortable home, one that fills all of my needs and is a pleasure to be in.

I fill the rooms with the vibration of love so that all who enter, myself included, will feel this love and be nurtured by it.

I love myself so I work at a job that I truly enjoy doing, one that uses all of my talents and abilities, working with and for people that I love and love me, and earning a good income.

I love myself, therefore I behave in a loving way to all people for I know that that which I give out returns to me multiplied.

I only attract loving people into my life for they are a mirror of what I am.

I love myself therefore I forgive and totally release the past and all past experiences and I am free.

I love myself therefore I love totally in the now, experiencing each moment as good and knowing that my future is bright and joyous and secure, for I am a beloved child of the Universe and the Universe lovingly takes care of me now and forever more.

And so it is.

Do you feel the energy in those words? Even typing this for you now opens up my heart and I feel that glow again. It brings me right back to a place where I had to have courage and trust that the changes I was implementing in my life were for the greater good of me and my young growing family.

These words also helped me tap straight into the most powerful energy of all – loving intention.

I would like to share with you a story about something that happened around this time. I was invited to a guided meditation with my beautiful forever friend, Donna. As a mum of a young family I rarely left my children so I could do things in the evening. I don't know why but on this occasion I felt as though I had to go, so with no expectation I arrived at the beautiful home of the person leading the meditation. It was my first ever meditation but oh my goodness what we all witnessed and felt through me was unbelievable.

The room had a beautiful energy. There were four of us there that night. I sat closest to the door and after a friendly chit chat we were guided into a meditation. I am not good at calming my mind, it is always active, but I did try, not knowing what I was supposed to be thinking, or not thinking for that matter, so I decided to listen to the tape that was playing. It was the voice of a man of Oriental origin. His words were calm, clear and powerful, they entrapped me straight away and I was being brought deep within myself. He worked from the busy mind, right down the face, neck and chest and stopped at the heart, where he talked about opening up the protective shield and feeling safe to let the love flow. WOW, WOW, WOW! A physical rush pulsated from my heart and I could feel the energy pulsating from my body so intensely. I felt like an electric pole radiating. I connected this feeling to the heart rushes I had sought medical attention for in previous months. This release was so intense it brought me to tears. The realisation was clear: I am a loving person and I had been protecting myself from living a love-filled life because of fear and circumstance.

After the meditation we sat and chatted. I didn't have to say anything, everyone had felt my energy. We were then asked to sit with a piece of one of the other people's jewellery in our hands and relay any messages that came to us. I had never done anything like this before but when I sat with a chain in my hand I got such an intense pain in my ear that I had to put the chain down. The pain stopped. I had no words though, but shared my experience with the chain's owner. One week later my friend told me the necklace owner's granddaughter was rushed to emergency the night of the meditation with a ruptured eardrum. Had I not mentioned the ear pain I experienced on holding her chain, she might have treated it with Nurofen when in fact it needed urgent medical attention.

For a few months previous I had visited the doctor with heart rushes. I didn't know what was happening to my body and was put on a monitor for a few days to test my heart rates. All tests came back normal and I was relieved.

I share this story because my mindset had a part to play in how much this impacted on my life. The emotion I felt while I was at the meditation was something I could not ignore. It shifted my perspective on life and in turn was instrumental in implementing change in my life.

What should I think about during meditation?

'The point of mindfulness is to learn to observe thoughts instead of getting caught up in them, so try to allow thoughts to come and go without getting lost.'
Oli Doyle

LIVE YOUR DREAM NOW, NOT IN THE FUTURE

There is a golden rule when it comes to attraction. You ask for it now, you feel like you have it now and you will manifest it now in this moment, then it will create your future. The key to this is to believe it in the *now*. It is a *fake it until you make it* type of attitude. Feel it now to become it later.

One of the key elements to this being successful is to embrace the journey of manifestation. It is important not to live in the future or for the future, it is most important to live and embrace the magnificence of the now.

Feeling the essence of something while setting a clear intention is an all-powerful approach to manifesting.

I have tested this approach and it is totally achievable. One fundamental element is that you have got to make your actions align with those of your future self.

The tools you need to achieve this are:

- Confidence
- Humility
- Peripheral power switched on
- Clear intention
- Stamina
- Courage
- Belief

To create a dream life you must not only plan for your future, you must live in the present. The future is always ahead, whereas the now is where the action takes place.

It is important to have your nearest and dearest on board. If they are more of a brick wall, there are ways of overcoming that without a visit to the divorce courts. But do let them know what your intention is so they are aware of the purpose for your distraction.

In 2010 I decided to set the intention to write a book. It was the most bizarre thing for me to choose to do as I had just had my fourth child, but because I had become increasingly aware of some powerful signs that presented themselves to me at the time I kept an open mind.

I had always deep down wanted to write a book, I had even paid for a comprehensive writing course. My tutor mentioned I was a philosophical writer and the funny thing about that was that I had no clue what that meant at the time and had to Google it. I was really impressed with myself and embraced it as it was something that came naturally to me.

The first sign was that some of my blog posts had been picked up by *Universal Mind*. The producer connected with me and asked if she could publish some of my articles in her monthly magazine. Secondly, I was watching the TV program *The View* and knew I was to watch the next five minutes of the show.

There were two special guests on that day, a reality TV couple who had publicly had many miscarriages through IVF. Whoopi Goldberg stopped the show and turned to the woman saying, 'I am going to tell you what I tell all of my friends when they endure this painful loss. You endured this for a reason, you are not on the right path in life. This was a visitor coming to tell you to get on the right path and your gift will come.'

That moment was like an epiphany for me. Two and a half years earlier I had endured a double miscarriage. It was the saddest experience of my life but it did knock me back onto the right track. I felt compelled to share this realisation with others who needed to hear it. It was an all-consuming feeling. I wrote a blog about it and it was published on the website I was writing for at the time. Then something came to my attention that I couldn't get out of my mind. It was NaNoWriMo, an annual writing competition where you pledged to write 50000 words during November. Broken down this was 1667 words a day and at the end you would have a book. I was filled with the possibility that I could actually do that.

I told my hubby my intentions and I had his support so I signed up. I was two days out from beginning and hadn't got a book in my head to write about. I sat down and wrote *The Visitor* on a page and all of these ideas came flooding out. In no time at all I had twenty possible chapters, some characters, a possible plot and theme but no specific genre, simply the *Knowing* that I had to do this. So armed with the will I found a way, and thirty days later I had written 51000 words. My NaNoWriMo graph shows that every day I wrote 1667 words. I know consistency was key to me completing this dream. I had the biggest sense of achievement. I had taken action and worked hard to achieve my dream.

I had worked the Law of Attraction and didn't even know it!

What I had also realised was that I did it with loving intention. My heart was one hundred percent open and it was a very heart-centred project. When I used the Law of Attraction and my loving intention, magic happened. This has come to be the essence of how I have made so much magic happen in my life. I focus on what is amazing and within my control and I embrace it with all of my heart.

Living in the now and making the most of every mindful moment guarantees we will have many more magic moments in the future. Believe me I have tested it so many times! I don't want to wait until the future to be happy, I want to be happy now so I make sure I express gratitude for everything I have, because I am truly grateful for all of my blessings. I one hundred percent believe that when we embrace the magic in our now, we will have more magic than we know what to do with in our future.

PERIPHERAL PERSPECTIVE

When you hear this saying, what comes to mind?

Peripheral power is the ability to see the wider picture, to embrace opportunities as they come from unexpected sources.

I have discovered that quite often we set an intention and then have a rigid plan in place of how the intention will come to fruition. I have news for you. That is not how the Law of Attraction works.

It is your job to set an intention and then act upon the opportunities that come.

I would not have built Serenity Press up to what it is today without having my peripheral power switched on. I set the intention to publish books and trusted I would be guided through each step and I was. I could never in a million years have predicted the journey Serenity Press has taken. Every incremental step was taken out of a *Knowing* and a desire to let it grow organically. Every time I needed to upskill I faced a challenge and set out to learn what I needed to so that I could reach the next step. It takes money to grow a publishing company and I am delighted I have taken the approach of offering services to raise the funds needed to grow my business. This takes courage, determination and trust to achieve.

Just before an interview about the Serenity Press new release *Writing the Dream*, Cheryl Akle from *Better Reading* magazine asked me a question that made me realise why the business has made it.

'Karen,' she said as we sat chatting on the rooftop of her hotel in Perth, with its wonderful perspective on the city, 'it takes money to run a traditional publishing press. How do you do it?'

No one had ever asked me that before, but I knew Cheryl had an insight into the publishing industry and I had better have a good answer. So my on the spot response was to tell the truth. 'Yes it does, Cheryl and the fascinating thing is that every time I needed to raise cash flow for the business an opportunity would occur and the cash I needed would be raised. Where there is a will, there is always a way.'

At the time I answered this question we were waiting for our shipment of *Writing the Dream* to arrive from Shanghai and it was late. We were not going to meet our deadline but somehow I knew it would be okay, and it was.

Peripheral power is another super power that some people may take for granted and others may not know how to use. By seeing the wider picture you will not miss opportunities for advancement.

ANYTHING IS POSSIBLE

'If you want to achieve you have got to believe.'
Karen Weaver, Job Buddies

This quote is taken from a children's book I wrote called *Alphabet Job Buddies*. It was the first thing I ever wrote for my children and it has been on a journey. It has a jingle that goes like this:

> *You can be whatever you want to be, if you try very hard then you will see that you can be so happy and your heart can be filled with glee.*

My children still sing this jingle even though years have passed since I first introduced them to it. It gives them a warm feeling and they know I wrote it for them.

Believing in yourself is something we gift to others, especially our children, but do we do the same for ourselves? Do you expect belief to come from an outside source? When you shift your mindset slightly to realise that the belief first needs to come from within, it is then that you will start the ball rolling towards success.

You have the power, don't give it to someone else.

Anything is possible!

The only limitations are those we impose on ourselves. I have tested the Law of Attraction many times safely within my personal limitations. I am an adventurous person at heart and as my motto is, *Where there is a will there is always a way,* I am open to many possibilities.

In 2015 I realised I had been so busy having babies and building a publishing press that I hadn't been back to Ireland to see my family since my move to Australia in 2008. I set the intention to get home but did not know how this would materialise. Knowing how the Law of Attraction works I didn't stress about that, I set the strongest loving intention that I could and nurtured that seed. I identified what my biggest block was and I set out to unblock it, in a loving way of course. I always find that when you choose to unblock in a loving way there is the possibility of damage limitation.

My mum hadn't come to visit when I had my sixth child for a few reasons, one being that she was still regaining her strength from having half of her lung removed (she is the strongest woman I know!). I simply had to see her but the reality was that I had five children under ten and my husband was busy working away. I wasn't prepared to wait another few years so when I saw there was a Qantas sale I did what I could to secure flight tickets in my price range to get us to Ireland and back and it happened. I set the intention and followed it through and it was happening. I actually turned it into a business trip as time and circumstance aligned to allow magic to happen.

During this trip I met with the newly appointed Earl of Crom Castle to chat about a potential writers' retreat. Within the next year I was back in Ireland hosting the retreat at the castle. It was the most amazing experience and a really good example of how you can make the Law of Attraction work for you if you set the intention and act on the opportunities that present themselves.

KIND ENERGY

Kindness doesn't cost anything but it can be the best investment you will ever make.

I cannot even begin to share the number of times kindness has paid off for me. It is a mindset choice that is truly magical. The energy created through being kind is gentle and so inviting for others. It is detected from a distance and appreciated on so many levels by others.

For the giver, happiness is never far away from kindness.

> **'Happiness is not something readymade.**
> **It comes from your own actions.'**
> *Dalai Lama.*

Kindness may not be the sexiest of all actions but don't underestimate its potential to have a profound impact on your life.

I really enjoy being kind. I like to be a ray of kindness into someone's day. It helps people reconnect with others instead of withdrawing. Kindness is what communities are built upon. *Be kind to thy neighbour.*

I grew up in a close-knit community until I was nine. Neighbours would watch out for each other's children and there was a sense of compassion and unity within that community. It's an amazing feeling to gift someone because it is not something that is expected, it is something that is gifted.

The sense of community is not as freely given now. I believe that stems from fear and not taking the time to get to know who your neighbor is anymore. I am blessed that I live on a street in Western Australia where my neighbor hangs bags of vegetables over the fence for my family. He gives without expectation of return but I know that someday I will repay him tenfold for the random acts of kindness he gifts our family. When he does it, it makes my day and I am so grateful. And as gratitude is one of the best ways to navigate onto the flow of abundance it is more than vegetables that he is sharing with my family.

I am a great believer that world peace can be achieved through kindness. Love is stronger than hate but quieter. When random acts of kindness make the news a wave of kindness ripples through society and yet news channels often choose to share news that is negatively focused, news that spreads fear and sadness. I find it sad that good news is not as commercial.

If we focus on what we can do ourselves, no matter how small, it will have a ripple effect that will soon become a tsunami of kindness that has the potential to instigate positive action in our world.

If everyone adopted a mindset that love, compassion and kindness were superpowers and set about using them daily, imagine how different the world would be. It's a nice prospect.

ABSOLUTE ABUNDANCE

'Money makes the world go around.' Well no, it doesn't, love does, but if you love money then you will have plenty of it.

You see, what you love most is what you will receive most of. If you are like me, money will not be the top of your list of priorities when in fact it should be, because with money I can make magic happen in my life, the life of my family and the lives of others.

We all deserve to experience financial abundance in our lives and we all can, but most of us don't want to sacrifice what we have in abundance (family love, lifestyle etc) to get it. However you don't have to. If you shift your mindset to becoming more open to receiving in a softer way, you can make a difference and not feel like you are compromising your life but enhancing it in a positive way.

This can be done through affirmations that will gently assist you in creating financial energy that will open up the channels of receiving money.

I have recently tested this and it worked. Being in the publishing world, projects need financing. I am usually good at moving forward and have a positive outlook on cash flow and building a business, but at this point I felt stuck and the cash had stopped flowing, which can be really tough for a business needing to do big things. I was also busy and doing lots, so my focus was scattered. I decided to take a day off and refocus my energy on creating wealth for my business. I sat with the loving intention of growing and I read the following affirmations from *The Secret* wealth app:

I am happy to give because my abundance is limitless.

I attract all that I need to bring forth my success.

I am a wealth creator.

I am using money to bless my life and other people's lives.

Every day in every way my wealth is increasing.

I am excited by other people receiving money.

The Universe conspires to give me everything I need.

I thank the Universe for all the prosperity that is mine today.

I am financially thriving.

There is an abundance of money and it's on its way to me.

I am receiving more money today.

I always have more money coming in than going out.

I love money and money loves me.

I am generous with money.

I am excited to see where more money is going to come from next.

The key to having more money is to feel like you have more money right now, in this very moment. This can be really tough if you are in debt or money is limited, but I can promise you that if you commit to being mindful about the money energy you are sending out into the Universe, your money story will change.

After one day of doing this I was receiving enquiries for new projects, had new ideas coming to me to act upon and even money that was outstanding found its way to the business.

This is relevant for business and home life. I suggest you put energy into making debt not feel like debt. The debt trap will only be a trap if you allow it to be.

Be grateful every day for everything you have. No matter how small it is, feel gratitude for it. Gratitude has instant access to the flow of abundance.

When you want to accumulate wealth, fill your mind with wealthy thoughts, feel wealthy when you think about money. Trick your mind into feeling wealthy and wealth will follow. The Law of Attraction works by giving you what you think about most, so it is important that when you think about money you are emitting a positive abundant energy to allow it to flow freely to you.

MONEY MINDSET

An abundant mindset that is mindful of the Law of Attraction is when someone consistently thinks prosperous thoughts irrespective of their actual situation and in turn manifests prosperity in the future because 'like attracts like'. Conversely, if a person consistently thinks they are poor then that will be their future experience.

One example comes from my LinkedIn friend Lisa Nichols, who is part of the film *The Secret*. She shares that '*Every time you look inside your mail expecting to see a bill, guess what? It'll be there. Each day you go out dreading the bill, you're never expecting anything great, you're thinking about debt, you're expecting debt. So debt must show up...it showed up, because the Law of Attraction is always being obedient to your thoughts.*'

Feeling happy and grateful for the money you already have is the fastest way to bring more money into your life.

It is a total shift in perspective about money and is well worth the effort, not only to increase financial wellbeing but to enhance emotional and health wellbeing. It is a win/win scenario and that is why New Age thoughts have been embraced wholeheartedly.

It can be quite tricky to manage if you are not a full believer. But when you entrust some of your energy towards it and begin to see results, it makes it easier to realise it is not a coincidence that you are actually using the power of your mindset to create money magic in your life. When opportunities you would never have considered start coming your way, it is then that you will truly begin to trust that there is a powerful connection to the energy flow of abundance. You can even play around with it and have a little fun. The key is to gain confidence and watch as it happens. But always remember it is your job to set the intention of wanting more money in your life. It is your job to feel wealthier, allowing it to flow to you, but it is not your job to know how it will present itself to you. So be open to opportunities and if they feel right for you, then go for it.

'People who have drawn wealth into their lives used The Secret, whether consciously or unconsciously. They think thoughts of abundance and wealth, and they do not allow any contradictory thoughts to take root in their minds.'
Rhonda Byrne.

IF LIKE ATTRACTS LIKE, KIND ATTRACTS KIND

'The game of life is a game of boomerangs. Our thoughts, deeds
and words return to us sooner or later
with astounding accuracy.'
Florence Scovel Shinn

Even though we cannot control what comes into our life we can choose what we act upon. When we react to something an energy is created from that action. When we purposely choose to set our mindset to respond in a kind and loving way it is amazing to watch the response of others.

This mindful approach works really well with children, they are very receptive to it and flourish because of that.

Some adults are less open to the concept, quite often due to their life experiences. When you are approached with negativity and respond with kindness, quite often the response to that will be criticism but know that you will have left a lasting impact, something for the person to think about. It may even be a catalyst for them to look at their behaviour. It is a human instinct to defend against threats so responding with kindness and compassion often has to be consciously learned but it is really worth it to watch it in action.

'Kindness is always an option. Choose it.'
Dalai Lama

The Dalai Lama lives and breathes kindness and compassion. The energy created from that has an immediate impact that makes the haters be still. He often speaks of the importance of discipline to live a peaceful life.

'A disciplined mind leads to happiness,
and an undisciplined mind leads to suffering.'
Dalai Lama.

A lot of what he shares is filled with divine wisdom and comes from a source of kindness. It is worth exploring the Dalai Lama's quotes if you wish to embrace kindness.

Remember, what you give out is often what you get back. Would you choose kindness if it was an option?

LOVE, THE HEALER

Love is the most powerful healer of all.

The one thing I keep coming back to for this is Louise Hay's *Heal Your Life*. This book is life changing.

It is written through the channel of loving intention and at the back there is a reference section that details the spiritual reasoning for physical ailments. I was shocked when I discovered the reasoning for lower back pain is financial worry. Funnily enough my husband suffers from severe back pain at times and he has become accustomed to now asking, 'What have you been spending?' I did set on a quest to get him to say the affirmations that would ultimately eliminate the negative thought pattern at the source of the problem but found that you can lead a horse to water…

Another explanation that intrigued me was that cancer is caused by holding on to resentment as it eats away at the spirit just as it eats away at the body. Dr Siegal who wrote *Love, medicine and miracles* suggests that traumatic events are precursors for cancer and he asks, 'What happened in your life in the two years before diagnosis?'

Louise Hay has had first-hand experience in curing her cancer by putting her philosophies to the test. She developed an intensive program of affirmations, visualisations, nutritional cleansing and psychotherapy to cure herself and in 1984 she released *You can Heal your Life*. I am a great believer in the power of the mind to heal. I also believe in the loving intention the medical profession has put into creating cures and performing surgeries, and that combined with the power of positive thoughts, healing will be at an accelerated rate. We are not all Louise Hays with such self control and natural knowledge so it is best to take advantage of maximum healing options.

My father suffered two strokes one year apart shortly after I moved to Australia. I had just had a baby and moved to a new country and felt the distance intensely at the time. My father has always been a very strong man and to think of him weakened crippled my heart. I have always been very close to him also, which intensified it even more. But amazingly, one year later he hopped on a plane and came to visit us. This was the best thing ever! To see how much he had healed was amazing. My dad has always been a person who 'gets on with it' and who has a bubbly character. He rarely got sick and when he did he would quietly heal and move on. Another year later and he had a consultation and MRI that astounded the doctors. His brain had fully healed, there was no sign of any scarring. Now my grandfather had early strokes and he sat by a fire all day and the strokes became something that defined him, but my dad wasn't prepared to do that. He wanted to drive again, he wanted to heal so much so he focused all of his energy on it and he did. He didn't do it alone, he had our whole family sending love and helping out as much as we could.

Love is an amazing healer. The energy created from the loving vibration emitted is all powerful. Look at a mother's love, it has the biggest healing potential of all. If my kids graze a knee or are really ill with a temp, it is my healing hugs that make them feel better, accelerating the healing process.

So the next time you are unwell and head off to the doctor or the chemist, consider also exploring the emotional trigger that caused the health problem and look at resolving the root of it so it doesn't present itself again.

Good health is my divine right. I am open and receptive to all the healing energies in the universe. I know that every cell in my body is intelligent and knows how to heal itself. My body is always working toward perfect health. I now release any and all impediments to my perfect healing.

Louise Hay affirmation

LET ALL THAT YOU DO
BE DONE IN LOVE

It's written in the Bible, so why do we not instantly do it? I expect it is because we are human and our minds are so complex. We like to over complicate things for ourselves and that's fine, but imagine a life where there was more space and things were simpler and much brighter. That is a life led through the heart.

You know those people who wear their hearts on their sleeves? I am one of those people but I have learned how to instantly shield myself from negativity. You know that Wonder Woman shield, ready for battle at any moment? It helps you when facing fearful situations because you will have confidence in the *knowing* that your heart is safe.

There is no pain as intense as a broken heart.

I know this first hand but I refuse to live a life fearful of experiencing this pain again. Instead I chose to be brave and put loving energy out into the world, fearless of the consequences. Love is confronting for some people but with those who embrace it, I have deep lasting connections.

The key to this is intention. I am passionate about the intention of people I meet. I often find myself silently questioning their intention for pursuing or saying things. I do have empathy for people who have been through a lot and who have underlying issues that lead to choosing negativity, but it comes back to the matter of choice. We can choose what we let define our lives, we can choose love, we can choose happiness or we can choose the opposite. It is all a matter of choice. I went through a rough time in my life and I became an introvert for a while, it was my choice and something I needed to do at the time. It was a dull place for me and I never felt at home there but I did emerge from it and chose to live a love-filled life that serves me so well. I could have chosen a very different path and I am so glad I chose love.

The easiest way to begin, if you haven't already, is to become more mindful of your intentions and in turn your actions. The act of giving is something special indeed and when executed without expectation it releases the disappointment that may follow, while also enhancing the experience of heartfelt gratitude when it comes.

It makes so much sense to pursue everything with loving intention. The results will be more than you could ever imagine and will come to you so much faster. Love is my go-to intention and so it comes very naturally to me. It can be the same for you with a little mindful focus.

I suggest you start small with things that are familiar and safe and then begin to find the courage to push the boundaries safely out of your comfort zone. You can even experiment and have fun with it all. I did. It makes it all so different when you do it with the *Knowing* that you are safely surrounded by love.

The Power
of Knowing

*The only true wisdom is in
knowing you know nothing.*

SOCRATES

THE KNOWING STRATEGY

So how does it work?

I use one strategy in manifesting everything in my life – the *Knowing* strategy. When I don't use this strategy I make mistakes and experience unnecessary and often costly detours when working towards achieving my dreams and goals. Destiny is there for us all to embrace but many of us settle with playing safe or get so distracted by the dazzling attraction of external objects that we waste time in reaching our highest potential.

It is when we reach our highest potential that the race for success ends and a new more relaxed pace of life is there for us to embrace if that is what we choose. There is profound comfort in the *Knowing* that you have succeeded in manifesting a deep-rooted desire, that all of your hard work and risk-taking has paid off. It is from this position that the world is your oyster and you can stand confident in the *Knowing* that you have made magic happen and can do it again if you so choose.

So, what is this *Knowing* strategy?

There are three simple steps.
1. Feel it.
2. Think it.
3. Achieve it.

Often a *Knowing* is understood to be an intuition. It isn't, although the channel of intuition plays an important role in *Knowing*. True *Knowing* goes deeper than intuition, it takes it to the next level. Intuition is often perceived as a feminine quality and because it is channelled through the frequency of love it is often more easily accessed by women. However, *Knowing* is something we all have the key to unlock. Through this book you will discover how to access YOUR *Knowing*.

Understanding the power in a *Knowing* is a life skill. One that you will develop to become increasingly aware when a message is reaching you and instinctively act upon it with the three-step strategy that I will talk about numerous times throughout this book.

This is often from an external source. Keeping open and aware is imperative. Successfully receiving and processing messages is vital.

KNOWING — HOW DO YOU PREPARE FOR IT ALL?

If your life is already full then be mindful that things will have to shift to allow the new to enter. It is often good to do a life declutter when setting an intention. I do it all the time. I start to feel overwhelmed and constrained so I begin to shift my focus to clear the backlog and avoid filling that void with more work. In doing so I create the space required for the magic to happen.

If you have already read Book 1 in this series, *Mindful Magic*, you will understand the principle of true magic happening when you create the space to let it in. How can it shine into your life if your life is at capacity, bursting at the seams?

Clearing the way ensures you will be able to channel your *Knowing* effectively.

How to declutter:

1. Write a list of everything you have filling your life right now. EVERYTHING!
2. Prioritise your list into three categories: what you want to do, what you must see through now and what can go.
3. For the least important list start imagining what it would be like to clear those tasks from your schedule. Imagine the space it would make in your life.
4. Do not plan to fill that space, keep it open until the right opportunities come your way. Fill the extra time with soul- nourishing activities.
5. Repeat every six months.

WHAT I MUST DO	WHAT I CAN DELEGATE	WHAT CAN GO

FEEL IT

You have probably heard how your feelings will help you generate the energy required to attract what you want. We have the power to control our feelings so we can manipulate our destiny and attract any number of desires. I have used this successfully on many occasions. So how is *Knowing* different?

Knowing is your internal compass, a skill you were born with and can access anytime. It's true power in the alignment with your true purpose and highest potential. It's the next level from *The Secret* by the wonderful Rhonda Byrne. It is having true ownership of who you were, are and choose to become. Watching *The Secret* kick-started my experience of being responsible for my thoughts.

Watching Louise Hay's *You Can Heal Your Life* gifted me permission to be loving and gentle and still make amazing things happen in my life through navigating my thoughts. It's all physics in the end and it is important to realise the impact your thoughts and feelings have on your world and the world around you. It is within your reach to influence those thoughts and feelings so you can live your best life and in doing so, do your bit to help others live theirs. It's all about choice.

Mastering the Law of Attraction can attract wonderful opportunities to you. I have become so in tune with this frequency that sometimes I am afraid to think because I instantly set in motion channelling whatever my heart desires.

This shouldn't be a problem but it can be, because it is my mind doing the desiring, not my soul. My soul is connected to my divinity, my true purpose, the purpose that makes my heart sing. My mind will not know what that is until it presents itself to me, therefore

I can mindfully manifest something that is not truly aligned or destined for me. That is where *Knowing* comes into play.

The first step of *Knowing* is to Feel It. When an opportunity is presented to you, how do you feel? Do you want to grab it straight away and run with it? If the answer is *yes*, that is wonderful. It is so exciting when bright shiny new opportunities come into our lives. It is at this point when you can instinctively move to the next stage of the *Knowing* process, which is to Think It.

I am not suggesting you talk yourself out of the opportunity. This step is simply asking yourself, 'Is this aligned with my divine purpose?' If the answer is *no* then walk away, because it is a distraction that will waste your time on your journey to your highest potential. Your highest potential is the journey you want to be on as it is the most fun, least stressful and the destination is somewhere you will never want to leave.

If the answer is *yes*, then you move to the next step, Action It. This could be simply saying *yes* or it may be pursuing a lead, completing an application or following through on a thought.

In my experience, when I have an inspired thought, I feel I need to take action right in that moment. That is generally a get-straight-on-to-it *Knowing*. Magic can happen when you act on that.

In December 2015 Oprah came to Australia. I booked tickets for myself and my beautiful friend Donna. If I was going to experience Oprah, I wanted her to be with me. Luckily she said yes and we were really looking forward to it. A week before the event an idea came to me that as Oprah is a book lover, a gift basket of books would be a fabulous gift for her. I was oblivious to all of the celebrity gifting companies that charge thousands of $$$ for the privilege, but I knew there was a way and I just had to find it.

I posted on Facebook to ask if any of my contacts knew anyone who worked at Perth Arena where the event was to be held. I got a reply and gave them a call. They guided me to the event management company that was coordinating the tour. Even though it was at the most inconvenient time for me I knew I had to call in that moment. I got through to someone who gave me an email address for the person in charge of the gifts. They emailed back with instructions to have the basket at a certain reception at a specific time.

Interestingly, that was the morning I was hosting the playgroup Christmas party at our school so on the day I delivered the basket dressed up as Santa's helper. It all made great PR. A lot of my entrepreneur friends heard about what I had achieved and reached out to ask if they could have my contact, which I shared freely but none of them got a reply.

I know that time and circumstance aligned to make that happen. I felt the opportunity, thought on whether it aligned with what I wanted to achieve, and finally took action in the very moment I needed to and magic happened.

When you are channelling your *Knowing* things happen fast so you need to be ready to act and know that it is aligned with what you are aiming to achieve. This was a fun time and I often get asked if Oprah ever contacted me. No, she didn't but I know that when time and circumstance align again, I can mention the gift basket she received at her first Australian venue and it will assist with a more meaningful interaction.

A *Knowing* generally goes against all logic, it is quite often the last thing you think you should be doing at that time in your life. It calls you and you must listen. It's important to remember that every event, interaction and moment in our lives is working towards our highest potential. It's that simple. The problem these days is that we get so distracted on the journey because there are so many possibilities.

It's the choices we make at those integral times that determine how long we will take to reach our destination. It is wonderful to have the privilege of choice because so many people have had that taken away from them as victims of circumstance.

In 2006 I went through a tough time. I suffered PTSD (Post Traumatic Stress Disorder) after a life event shifted my very being. The feeling of 'things will never be the same again' was something that shocked me to my core. I loved my life and juggled so many things. I didn't realise that it is then that things can crumble. Looking back I can see I wasn't identifying the signals happening around me. I wasn't being mindful and this life event occurred to set a ball in motion so I would take action and move forward towards my highest potential.

I always knew I was destined for more than small town living. It frustrated me a little because I would have loved to have been content in my heart to be still and live a simpler, less complicated life. The reality was that for me, that would probably never be the case. Moments of quiet, yes, I treasure them, especially when I am recharging my batteries ready for the next adventure. But content with stillness forever? No, not me. It isn't in my DNA. So, during my year and a half of stillness I took the time to consider moving to Australia. This is not something I would ever have considered beforehand. My mother and I had been to see a tea leaf reader and when she said that I would live in Australia, I totally blocked it because I was so close to my family there was no way I was going to not see them every day.

But the events that had occurred created the possibility in my mind so I applied for our residency visas for Australia. It took me one full month to collect all the paperwork we needed. I had to be determined and focused but I did it and then left it in the hands of faith, knowing that if this was to be, it would be.

A year later we still hadn't heard any word and were living in limbo, not knowing what action to take. But actually, we were taking action by being there in that moment preparing for it all. Life was aligned even though it wasn't good. There were things we needed to endure and experience to get us aligned with the divine timing of what we were about to do. I never lost the *Knowing* that this was what we were supposed to be doing. I remained focused on the goal and got on with aligning myself with it, even though there was no certainty. All I had was faith that everything was happening and when I needed to take action, I would *Know*.

We got our visa call at the very moment I was picking up our wedding rings from the jewellers. When things align like that they are affirmations that you are on the right track. We planned to leave on September 1st, the first day of spring in Australia and autumn in Ireland. I was thirty-five weeks pregnant with my third child. It looked to be the craziest thing to be doing in my life at that point as we had just completed building a new house and were locking it up to pursue the unknown. Yet I did know this was the very thing I was supposed to be doing. I never wavered or questioned the process; I just *Knew*.

I share stories like this because we can all learn from each other's stories. It felt as though my life was falling apart but it was actually coming together. I was gifted the unwavering *Knowing* that what I was doing was totally aligned with my highest purpose, even though at the time I did not know what that higher purpose was. Make sense?

It does take courage to have this type of unwavering faith in *Knowing* as quite often it goes against conventional thoughts and practices. Your courage to connect directly with YOUR source of purpose will be rewarded and save you heaps of time in the pursuit of your goals if you roll with it and take immediate action when you reach step three in the *Knowing* strategy.

Knowing and Your Why

'Knowing your deep WHY stimulates
your willpower for change'

Levi Newton

Many people grow up with restrictions. These restrictions are put in place by our parents, society and other sources and stem primarily from fear. This is fine but how are we supposed to learn to navigate our inbuilt protective system when we have been protected from using it for so long? This system is the Power of Knowing. *Knowing* when it is safe to act and *Knowing* that we are moving forward guided and protected from harm is a powerful internal instinct that so many people are not familiar with using due to external 'nannying'.

I know how it goes, I am guilty of this too. I am a mum of six and I feel it is my job to protect my little beings but I have become increasingly aware that it is more beneficial to them if I see my role from an alternative perspective. That is to guide them and part of that guidance is showing them how to connect with their *Knowing* because that life skill will protect them way beyond my gaze. *Knowing* when something is aligned and when it is the right time to take action is a gift to our little ones.

The ultimate goal for those who embrace *Knowing* is captured in that split-second moment where you have the unwavering ability to say yes or no.

Learning how to activate this tool and navigating it so it is always working aligned with your highest intention is a skill that can be developed.

Where do you get a Knowing? My dear friend, you already have it, we all do, but through the generations we have lost the natural ability needed to access it intuitively.

That is why this book is important and why we all need to learn how to *Know* again.

Personal power is something that is not treasured as it should be in this day and age. I am astounded that so many people are willing to hand over their power to others. Do you not realise that the power to make our own choices, walk our own path is worth so much more than any gold coin? We need to alter our perspective on what is valuable, where life's wealth truly resides. Believe me, you can have all the money in the world but that might come with huge burdens to bear.

Is it not ideal to walk our own path fulfilled because we *Know* we are aligned? The energy of feeling aligned is where life's magic happens. It is an undercurrent and you can see it in those who are truly aligned with their true purpose. They are comfortable in their own skin, glowing because they are living their best life for them; growing in spirit as well as in life.

We are human and it's normal to seek outwards for guidance, it is something we are conditioned to do. The problem with this is that when we do this, we also hand over our power, which is connected to the outcome of any given situation.

Think about babies. They cry out when they are in need of something but they don't give over their power; that remains their own. Yes, it is influenced by those who care for them but instinctively their goal is growth of mind, body and spirit and they do it well.

So why is power important?

This book is called The Power of Knowing because at the very core of *Knowing* is the realisation of the power we have to make unwavering choices in our lives. Choices that are fully aligned with where we are on our journey and our desired destination.

Opportunities present themselves daily. Many people struggle with making instant choices and they miss the real opportunities that have been snapped up by those who do have this ability.

It is about aligning yourself with your highest intention, an intention that is aligned with your soul purpose, so that when time and circumstance align for you, you are ready to say *yes*. This allows the flow of magic to happen.

Please know that aligning with your true WHY and then making it happen through a *Knowing* strategy is not selfish, in fact it is quite the contrary. Imagine a world where people answered their calling and pursued their purpose. Would that not be a divine world? Believe me, there will still be people who are happy to have uncomplicated jobs to make money because their priority is to live a simpler existence. That is fine. There will always be people who are starting out on the road to pursuing their purpose and so will do what is required to make that happen. But they will do it with gratitude, knowing it is a lever forward to activating their goal.

Once you pursue your purpose with loving intention then you will achieve it faster and even bring others along for the ride.

As Elizabeth Gilbert states in one of her posts whilst writing *Big Magic,* it is wonderful to pursue our passion once it doesn't harm someone else.

The benefits of living through your Why:
1. You live your life on purpose and aligned with the highest version of yourself.
2. You give your best to the world.
3. You will inspire others and show up as a leader in your realm.
4. When a 'why' is the essence of all intention, in there resides a power that is almighty.

Exercise: What is your Why?

Knowing and Your Relationship with Divine Energy

When writing this book, I endured a few blocks which hindered progress. I know when this happens in my books it is because something needs to be revealed. This doesn't help when your distributor is waiting for a delivery so with reluctance I put the book on hold and gave it the grace it needed to flow to me. *Knowing* is the second of my master gifts to live a life without fear and on purpose so I honoured the 'no fear' part and distracted myself with other projects until what needed to come to me did so.

Then one day I saw a post by one of my biz friends on Facebook about having a session with another of my biz friends, international psychic Rebecca Gibson. I am usually guided very confidently through my own *Knowing* and quite literally that is the reason for writing this book, but the call was loud and I *Knew* that Rebecca had something I needed to know. So I answered the call and booked a session. I imagine the energy between us was at very high levels because the internet was playing up. As we both live life on a high frequency that was to be expected. This was also our first face-to-face interaction — well, on Zoom.

We hit it off straight away and she asked me what questions I wanted to ask.

'What do I need to know?' I asked.

Watching this woman at work was wonderful. Rebecca spoke about my work and saw it exactly as it is and that I am very much at the core of it all. Then other questions began to flow and the final question came to me like a bolt of lightning so I asked about this book series.

'You need to connect with your relationship with God,' she said.

This caught me off guard but then it all became clear.

Knowing is all about having faith, living without fear. The penny dropped that our *Knowing* is at the essence of Godliness. We are the masters of what we achieve in life, we can make things happen and have so much more influence over our destiny than we even allow ourselves to comprehend. Sometimes this stems from conditioning and limiting beliefs that we are exposed to as we grew into who we are today. It is often easier to accept what we have been taught rather than challenge our own thoughts and have the courage to explore the internal calling wanting us to listen and navigate our personal path to our individual destiny. No two destinies will be the same because everyone walks a different path. We all have a different personality so even if the goal is the same, the formula for achieving it and the journey taken to reach that summit will be different. And as I always say, 'Everyone has a story to share because no two stories will be the same.'

The world has so many religions, all with a higher source that is honoured as a master of that religious orientation. It is always wonderful to have a positive loving leader who inspires masses of people to do beautiful things in the world but I can never get my head around any God inspiring people to come from a place of hate or revenge. This saddens me because I know these actions stem from fear and it is universally known that God does not live in fear. God lives in faith and hope and there is no fear associated with these actions. When you are filled with hope and are faithful that every step you take is aligned with your higher purpose, you will feel fulfilled and have no need to bring another person down. There really is enough for us all to share. Everyone has a different agenda and just because someone has something you want it doesn't mean there is any less for you.

If we morally eradicated greed and fear as a global motion and allowed everyone to be treated humanely; if we were all taught to deal with life's situations with loving intention, then conflict would not escalate to warfare. Harmony would ripple across the globe. One leader who embraces this type of leadership is New Zealand's

Prime Minister, Jacinda Ardern. How she dealt with a terrorist attack was amazing. There was no fear in her response, only love and sadness. Sadness for the loss and empathy for the pain of fellow humans whose lives were changed forever at the hands of another fellow human. She didn't speak his name and allow him the media exposure he probably hoped for. The world saw only the loving actions of a prime minister who leads with her heart; who is trusted by her constituents and who makes other leaders take notice that there may be another way to lead rather than through force.

God is a three-letter word that holds so much power and has been interpreted in so many ways by different religions and that is fine so long as it doesn't hurt someone else. I know God is almighty, a power so much bigger than anything we could ever comprehend. Individually we are unique beings so there is 'no one size fits all' religion; we have to embrace an authentic, deep-rooted connection within ourselves. Connect with who we truly are and then bespoke our relationship with God, so that our connection is divine.

My spirituality is individual, it isn't governed by a set of rules and regulations, it is authentic and love filled. Anything I do for another person I do out of genuine choice, because I want to, not because I feel I should. Your connection with God should be free-willed, not forced upon you by society or because you fear the repercussions of what your family chose to follow.

I grew up Catholic. My beloved granny was a devout Catholic, the beautiful church was at the end of our park and most of our teachers were nuns, with some priests in the later years. I attended school in Ireland in the 1980s and religious studies was a big thing. There were statues all around the school just as in the church. They were sacred and every school was named after a saint. We were slapped if we did something wrong. I cannot imagine what I would do if a teacher slapped one of my children in this day and age!

I was pretty good and quiet so I never got slapped but I do have the mental scars of witnessing others being slapped with meter rulers, or a teacher's ring being thumped into a shoulder. This is nothing compared to what my mother had to endure in the 1960s. The nuns would make her scrub floors instead of learn because she was from a lower class family in the community, instead of helping their family out, which I am sure would be God's will. The nuns would abuse the system and judge my mother and many others because of their family status. I don't believe God would discriminate. My mother never really brought us to church or spoke too much about the emotional and physical abuse she endured at school. I know shame was one emotion she felt and she over-compensated with her children; we never went without.

I share this because taking the opportunity to understand your roots and re-establish your connection with God will allow you to connect at a deeper level with divine energy, therefore having a deeper connection with the highest version of yourself. Sometimes it is a story that can be rewritten. *Knowing* is so much more effective when you know through the channel of unconditional love.

Have as much faith in yourself as you would in your beliefs. For you are the essence and power that comes with making miracles happen. When you focus that energy inwards you will be a better person to share with the world. Many of the big players are the biggest believers in themselves and others follow the journey.

Knowing and the Importance of Priorities

Do you know the importance of priorities? Do you know what your priorities are right now?

A conversation I heard from Elizabeth Gilbert in Perth helped me realise the importance of priorities in our lives. I have realised how important it is that we grow alongside our priorities and allow them in some sense to help us navigate our way through life. She said many people set intentions but they don't make them a priority. So how are they supposed to happen?

We can come up with all of the excuses under the sun for something not happening but I am going to call you out on it if you have not achieved an intention you have set. It is because you didn't prioritise it.

As for a lot of chapters in this book I will funnel my life experiences to the themes in discussion. Currently, we are going through the 2020 global pandemic and priorities have adjusted virtually overnight. My adjustment has not been too significant as I actually live every day connected to my home base. I do have an office and enjoy the division it gifts me between work and home life. However, setting up a makeshift office at home again isn't an issue for me because that's how I roll during school holidays anyway. It isn't ideal but I get on with it because being there for my kids when they are young is a priority for me, a choice.

I am not saying the global pandemic has forced people to succumb to unwanted priorities; in fact, I am saying the opposite. It has been a true gift to many to reset their priorities and be gifted the time for their mindset to adjust. Isolation may seem like torture for some and yet many people choose to isolate regularly without a pandemic because it gifts them time to go through the motions of adjustment.

I know when I am evolving or making a choice to change an

element of my life, I set the intention and prioritise any adjustments that need to happen. When things are changing around you it can feel very unsettling as the cogs and wheels of your familiar life begin to adjust speed and fine tune to your new speed. That's okay and you will allow it to happen when you are aware of what's happening. But if you are not an aware person it can feel like your world is falling out from underneath you. In this case it can make a person resist or fear any outcome because faith is required during this process and there are no guarantees with faith!

Faith is the essence of *Knowing*. Have you ever watched someone who is going through something huge and thought, 'Wow, if that was me I would be all over the place?' Yet they are just going through the motions of it, confident of the outcome. That is *Knowing* in action. I can assure you that person does not know exactly what the outcome will be but they have faith in the process. They set a powerful intention for their goal to happen and prioritised it in their life. When they do this through their *Knowing* they understand the next step will present itself and they will know what action to prioritise to achieve the greatest outcome. Feel It, Think It, Action It!

**"It is not a daily increase, but a daily decrease.
Hack away at the inessentials."**
Bruce Lee

When you start to build traction on your path your priorities become more important. I have had to adjust priorities along the way and find new ways of managing what I love best, which is to help stories find their way into the world. After reading *Do Less, Be More* by Susan Pearse I stopped spreading myself thin teaching the same thing over and again and instead thought outside the box. How could I serve more people more efficiently? It was then the Everything Publishing Academy was born. I put a lot of content and energy into the academy and had an amazing bunch of people in there. I did this for a couple of years and when it was flowing along nicely and not needing me so much, I chose to prioritise my personal passion for sharing my thoughts in this book series. I founded my Life Magic group and in 2020 we have been doing a gratitude challenge where every day I post a graphic and share what I am grateful for that day. It is a beautiful energy and many of the group share what they are grateful for each day too.

Have you visited your priorities recently?

Are your priorities your choice?

Many of us choose to be parents and gift a lot of our time to nurturing our children to adulthood. Yes, it's hard work but a choice and we prioritise that. Many of us choose to build a career or take on a job and make that a priority too and that is fine also. These are not sacrifices, they are choices and the hard work associated with them and all of our priorities are our choices. The priorities I would like you to revisit are those that are not your choice and no longer serve you.

> **'Things which matter most must never be**
> **at the mercy of things which matter least.'**
> *Johann Wolfgang von Goethe*

We need to regularly check in with what we prioritise in our life because as we grow we outgrow a lot. Just because you prioritised something last year or five years ago doesn't mean you have to keep it a priority for a lifetime. If you want to, then that's wonderful but if something is only a priority for a season of your life it is important that you set it free so it can find its way to someone else who will value it.

Personally, I feel too many people don't prioritise themselves and it leads to a lot of resentment and disconnection. Prioritising yourself is not selfish, it is vital for a harmonious society. When you meet your own needs it means you have the best of you to give to others. I truly believe this with all of my heart. If you want to live a life filled with life magic, which I hope you do because you are reading the Life Magic series, then I suggest you prioritise your interests because they are more important than you will ever know.

What are your priorities now?
What can you move away from?
What do you choose to prioritise in the future?

**'Most of us spend too much time on what is urgent
and not enough time on what is important.'**
Stephen R. Covey

THINK IT

The second stage of the Knowing process is vital as it harmonises the feminine Feeling It (intuition) and the masculine Thinking It. Individually they are strong but together they are powerful.

So how do you embrace the thinking associated with *Knowing*?

It's quite simple, you ask yourself one question:

'Is this aligned with my highest potential?'

If the answer is *no* or you need to think on it, then dismiss it because when you truly *Know* then you will instantly know when something is aligned.

If you are starting out on the process of truly *Knowing* then this can be a case of trial and error. Try not to be too hard on yourself because when something is destined for you, you will attract it right back through your intentions. I will chat more on this in Book 3 of the *Life Magic* series, *The Miracle of Intent*.

For now, get to know you, what you truly want to achieve, and feel into the journey of life that you want to take. When you honour your path, those who walk alongside you in life will benefit.

Try not to overthink the **Think It** part of the process. It isn't supposed to be complicated and always remember *there is no fear in Knowing*!

Knowing and Choice

Making choices comes naturally to some people and if that's you, well done. Embracing The Power of Knowing is more about embracing the principles of the process and making them a habit, which rewires your brain and becomes less of a push and pull scenario. Of course, in any breakthrough there is always a struggle beforehand so that you learn the skills needed to break through to the next level.

If you struggle with making choices, then you need to read this chapter!

Most people do not know they have the power over their own life. Yes, of course environmental, societal and global events affect our current circumstances, but it is a choice to be a victim of circumstance or the master of your own destiny no matter what is going on in the outer world. One thing is for sure, YOU are the master of YOUR world. Whether you want to hear it or not, you are responsible for where you are right now. And you are responsible for whether you choose to see that in a positive or negative light.

We all have challenges to endure in our lifetime, many inflicted upon us by external sources. When we find peace with knowing we cannot be responsible for others' actions, we can only be responsible for our own, then there is freedom in that. We can choose to forgive others, not for them but so that we are freed from the shackles of what could have been a lifetime of pain and a lifetime lost because it was defined by a past incident. Remember, the person you look at in the mirror now stands before you warts and all. That person needs you to show up, own your choices and move forward, stepping into the power of what can be, not what was.

You can choose in any moment to learn and evolve from the shadows of the past. I promise when you choose to step into the light you will shine brighter, you will evolve from a cocoon and when you are ready to spread your wings there is a big wide world filled with opportunities for you to behold.

There is enough for everyone on this planet, there is enough for you to have anything your heart desires.

Making choices that include your desires is not selfish, it is your duty to live a life filled with things you love. So long as what you do does not intentionally harm another person then go for it, life is for living to our highest potential.

The next time you have a choice to make, ensure that you feel into it first, then ask the golden question, 'Is this aligned with my highest potential?' and if the answer is *yes*, then find the courage to take immediate action.

There is always a perception about the way you should do something; often when you truly *know* you will discover that what you are being guided to do defies conventional thought practices. It's your choice which you choose.

Knowing and Your Calling

**'Choose a job you love, and you will never
have to work a day in your life.'**
Confucius

These words of Confucius ring so true to me now that I live through my passion for sharing stories with the world. This calling has seen me live a tremendous life and experience truly wonderful things that I could have only dreamed of before I took the steps forward to embark on this journey.

You see, I LOVE the journey, I love that I can get up every day and do what I love, it is kind of like I get to do my hobby every day! This got me thinking. Many people do jobs that don't fulfil them, not knowing what their calling is, or maybe not even realising that we all have a calling waiting for us to answer it. Our gift to the world is always a gift to ourselves and each gift is different. It is not a choice for our minds to make but more being open to something that presents as a possibility.

Have you ever thought on the word hobby? Do you think our hobby is actually our true calling in motion? Surely a hobby is something that fulfils us, makes us happy and something we could do all day long without watching the clock. So why do so many people choose to do a hobby in their 'spare time' as a reward for drudging through another work week? Why can't our hobbies be our jobs and our spare time be filled with hugs and time with our loved ones?

I choose the latter and have made my hobby (my calling) my job. Therefore I don't feel the need to fill my spare time with anything other than spending time with my nearest and dearest; also for walks and replenishing my energy so that I can show up as my best self, time and time again. I know I am privileged to live this life and I never take it for granted, not for one moment.

So is eradicating the unwanted job the answer we are all looking for? Do some self-discovery and make the choice for yourself. I know many people who are happy to clock in and clock out and not have to think about work again until the next time they have to clock in. That in itself is freedom. I have had those jobs in the past and they are very important jobs in society. There are many people who believe this is how things should be, when in fact that is not the case.

I invite you to think about your hobby and whether you are happy to keep it as something you do on the side, or if something more is calling you to act and upgrade your skills aligned with your passion.

Making the Choice to be Your Own Success Story

Listen to other success stories. Many of the storytellers, especially those who are connected to their divine purpose, talk about how they just *Knew* there was something they should do. Even though it defied logic they took the chance and it paid off. Yes, they had challenges to overcome but every challenge came at an integral point of their journey; a point when they were required to step up and evolve from where they were previously.

When you read such stories in their entirety you will easily identify the *Knowing* that was an integral point at the beginning of the writer's journey and then each stage along the way that required them to access their *Knowing* again. I guarantee they *felt it, thought it and actioned it*! It becomes an instant and integral part of any success story and it shows they weren't actually taking a chance at all but were aligned with actioning their highest potential. They couldn't fail once they chose to evolve through each challenge and take action through each aligned opportunity, disregarding the distractions along the way.

So how do you become your own success story? The answer is simple: you need to revisit your definition of success. I speak about this in Book 1 of this series, *The Magic of Mindfulness*. It all starts with you! Why? Because your success story may not be about how much money you have in the bank or how you build a business, your ultimate success story may be a goal or a journey or both. In Book 3, *The Miracle of Intention*, I share more on how to set and leverage intentions so they are perfectly aligned with how you navigate to your perfect destination. Right now learning how to use the Power of Knowing is important because before you set any intentions you should learn how to truly *Know*.

Part of that is to truly connect with the essence of who you are and what makes you tick. Identify what YOU want to achieve and realise that you will need to make room in your life for the magic of that to happen. Learning how to know again means you don't overthink things, you FEEL into them, that is your guide. You feel right in the depths of your soul that you want this, that this is aligned with your goals.

If you don't know your purpose just now, that is fine. If you don't know what you want to achieve, that is fine too.

What is important, and the reason I began this book with conversations with God and connecting with divine energy is because when you do, you exist on another level.

Given the level of success I have experienced to date you might be surprised to know I never knew what my purpose was until I accidentally stumbled upon it through a series of events. I believe way too much emphasis is put on the word 'PURPOSE' and there is too much stress to find what that is for us and pursue it for a lifetime.

If you focus on connecting with the divine energy within you, the power that you have to connect at a higher level in life, then you will FEEL your purpose. It is not something you think on, it is something you feel. I can quite confidently say, 'I am totally aligned with my purpose' and not because of the degrees I have or the blood, sweat, tears and thoughts I put into finding it. It all began when I got to know who I was and what made me shine from within. I can guarantee that it wasn't anything materialistic. It is always something that I connect with and that is individual.

I see so many people wasting their life pursuing success, slogging their way through challenge upon challenge and evolving into something that is not aligned with who they truly are on the inside. They lose themselves along the way and quite often turn into someone who is not very nice to others or to themselves. That is understandable because they are living against their inner alignment. They are living through thoughts alone, not thoughts aligned with feelings, which of course is way more powerful.

One interesting fact I came across on my journey is that our heart actually has a brain and that when our intuition is actioned, that feeling we have in our gut is a combination of heart and thoughts.

No matter at what point in your life you are reading this book, if you do not feel aligned with where you are at, I invite you to consider taking an emotional break from what you are doing. Go on an inner retreat and get to know the you that once shone. Reconnect with the essence of that person. Whether you choose to stop your current life in its tracks and go on a physical destination (hello *Eat, Pray, Love*) or change your current thought cycle by introducing a practice such as meditation, yoga, walks along the beach, gratitude or whatever else works for you to begin taking steps inwards, I encourage you to embrace it. Whatever brings you to the essence of you will lead you to being successful no matter what medium it is you choose to pursue.

I have too often seen the pursuit of unaligned success resulting in many wasted years in the gift of a lifetime.

ACTION IT

When taking action it is advised to do this through the intention of love. Loving intention is one of the fastest ways to receive what you seek.

Action It is the final part of the *Knowing* process. Taking action sets the wheels in motion. This is an important part of the process because through our actions we get a response from those around us.

Every action causes a reaction.

When actions are initiated through our power of *Knowing* we can feel confident in the decisions we are making and move forward confidently, knowing we are working towards our highest potential.

I know many people who are nervous about making decisions. Making a decision is often thought to be one of the most enormous things we do in life and yes, ultimately it is because every choice we make weaves our web of life. That is why making choices channelled through a *Knowing* will gift us the freedom to make choices that are aligned with our highest potential. Thus any setbacks or blocks come to help us grow and learn the skills we need to learn at that point to propel us forward.

Quite often people spend a lot of time covering their tracks or putting agreements in place as a precautionary measure so they won't be liable for their decisions if they prove to be wrong. And yes, I completely understand why this happens, we definitely need to protect ourselves from risk. However I believe The magical essence of the natural flow of progression and alignment is hindered in this type of scenario.

Pressing pause for a moment is fine with the flow of the Power of Knowing but when you stop and disconnect with the essence, the momentum will have been altered. And to be perfectly honest I am very passionate that when you *Know*, you *Know*. That means you learn to action things immediately if they are aligned otherwise you risk missing out on an opportunity.

Feel it, Think it, Action it.

If there is any hesitancy when you get to the stage of thinking, 'Is this aligned?' then the answer is *no*, because when you truly know, you don't hesitate. You will learn to action straight away.

The Golden Rules of Knowing

There are key rules to knowing:

1. **Honour your decisions.** Have no regrets for any decision to say no. You made the decision for a reason at that point in your life. Move on from it. If it keeps calling you back then when the time is right look into it again.

2. **Follow the three-step process.** Feel it, Think it, Action it. This should become an automatic ability and part of your daily life. Use it as part of your life ammunition when manifesting, making choices and embracing opportunities.

3. **Be at one with the essence of you.** When you do this you will be able to *Know* on a higher level and your life will automatically upgrade. You will have the opportunity to live life on your terms and aligned with who you deserve to become.

4. **Embrace the journey.** It's important to remember the value of the journey. So many people see it as a struggle, but it's not meant to be. When you are aligned the journey is an amazing experience that you never want to end. It goes on and on and the destination becomes less of a priority. This is Life Magic.

Knowing and Taking Action on Inspired Thoughts

There are lots of lessons and wisdom paths that I have walked and many knowing stories I can share. My story about a Duchess and a publisher seems to be one that people wish to hear.

I have always had an intention to build a traditional publishing press filled with amazing established writers producing beautiful books and also creating opportunities for emerging authors. I set the intention of building a million dollar press. I am a great believer that there is miracle in intention and that when we have the right love-filled intentions ANYTHING is possible.

One night I was checking in on my Facebook family and saw that Sarah, Duchess of York was at an event in London run by a friend of mine. I loved watching her speak her words of wisdom to an audience of business owners.

It popped into my head that my son loved her Budgie the Little Helicopter books when he was younger and this led me to an inspired thought: 'I wonder if the Duchess would like to write a book for Serenity Press?'

That inspired thought set a string of actions in motion. I sat with that powerful loving intention energy and searched for the Duchess's agent. I wrote an email and it must have been passed on through the agency to the Duchess's office. I received an email requesting more information about what I was proposing and eventually a call was set up.

One of the things I promised myself was to make the process easy and not create any blocks to the flow of it. So when the call was requested during the time I was away with five of my children I still said yes. The main lesson there is to make it as simple as possible for someone to say yes.

Ask without expectation and eradicate all fear from the equation. The moment I decided to send that email I promised myself to honour the journey that would evolve and stick with it through whatever presented itself.

It was a process of trust building and showcasing my own and my team's ability to get the job done. I believe that because the Duchess and her team had an open heart and mind and we aligned very much with that, then something magical would happen — and it has.

I remember the day when I was sent through a beautifully illustrated piece of paper from the Duchess. She had sat in her garden and written about an oak tree and sent it to me. I read it and was entranced! I wanted to bring this beautiful story to life and it has quickly become *The Enchanted Oak Tree*. This book was supposed to be the first book we published because it represented so much at the time and was such an integral part of the Duchess Serenity Series project coming together.

I hope you enjoyed this insight into how by following my *Knowing* I secured a publishing deal with a Duchess. Watch this space — divine timing is in motion.

Knowing Yourself — Go Within or Go Without

When *Knowing* becomes a habit it is something you will do without having to be too mindful of it. In order to do this, you must first get to know yourself and that requires you to take time to go within.

For many people that can be a scary prospect. When we go inward, everything we haven't dealt with is there waiting for us to address it. It's important to do this regularly as we move along in our life. Those who don't can suffer major illnesses due to the festering of what is simmering inside. We all deal with things differently and when we don't honour and release the emotions we have buried during the tough times I believe they can manifest as something else.

When I moved to Australia in 2008 I did not think for one moment that I had a whole suitcase of unwanted issues tucked away. Yet so many things I had not addressed through my thirty years of living began presenting themselves one by one. It was quite overwhelming at the beginning but I then found the power in honouring and releasing them one by one. I realised that when things happen and we are not in the mindset to deal with them, we tuck them away in a special place inside until our mind and body knows we have the strength to release them. Sometimes we can resist that process because we don't feel ready but from my experience it is about stepping outside your comfort zone. It was when I did that I began to write and it was a fabulous release for me.

The best time for this process is when we are detached from the full-blown emotion and on the road to healing. Perspective is an interesting thing. We react to the way we perceive things to be and we can look at these times as a setback or a breakthrough. When the emotion is honoured (and that may be by having a good cry, hitting a punching bag or running through every aspect of the event and processing it before releasing it out of your body) I see it as a breakthrough.

I discovered the power in writing about it. Writing is an action and therefore it transfers a thought to something tangible that can be managed. Thoughts are directly connected to feelings and therefore are harder to manage. That is why when we don't feel ready, we hide them in that internal box. It is when we don't empty the box that big implosions happen.

Having grown up in Northern Ireland during the last decade of the Troubles I know there are so many internal boxes overflowing and that is why mental health is such an issue. Perhaps if resources were targeted at showing people how to empty their box or at least declutter it, then we would not have a mental health epidemic.

It is in disconnecting with our Power of Knowing that this has become such a problem. Our Power of Knowing is our internal compass, navigating us through life. When we are in tune with it then we *Know* when we need to empty our box.

So how do we reconnect? It is all about being aware of the signs, or internal call and taking the time out to stop and address whatever is happening.

Many people do this automatically but others keep suppressing the need. It is about being aware of what type of person you are.

People who are givers often keep things hidden whereas more aggressive people are constantly releasing and so their box doesn't overflow as much. Yet the anger needs to stem from somewhere so those issues still need to be addressed.

Do you ever notice that it is often the most gorgeous people who get seriously ill?

Are you a person who releases as you go along, maybe through sports, journaling, meditating or other forms of expression? Or are you a person who brushes things under the carpet hoping that the dust blows away? But the dust doesn't blow away, it waits there building up until you take the time to address it and release it. So try to take the time to release pent up emotions. It is vital for your future health.

One of the go-to books I embrace when I feel an ailment coming on is Louise Hay's *You Can Heal Your Life*. I often mention it in my books because I believe in the science behind it. I like realising the spiritual reason for my dizziness, stomach pain, toothache or whatever is going on at any given time. That allows me to pair up medicinal treatment with self-awareness and deal with the issue from the root core. This type of self-exploration is very valuable when harnessing the power of knowing.

The Miracle
of Intent

Intention is the seed of all reality;
so if you want to change your reality and
discover your true potential, you need
to create a new intention.

ANDREW WALLACE

WHY IT IS IMPORTANT
TO SET INTENTIONS

People with BIG goals are the most alive people I know. I have always enjoyed setting intentions and seeing where life brings me in the pursuit of achieving those goals. I always feel truly alive, my core essence shines bright because I am on an epic adventure. Any adventurer will tell you that yes, the journey is hard work but every bit of it is worth it when you are working towards something you genuinely want to achieve. When I look back on what I have achieved in my life, it's amazing! I am astounded but not surprised by what I have achieved in eight years in business, because I don't see limitations. I set big intentions and pursue them with unwavering faith in my ability to *Know* what opportunities are aligned with my goals and what are not. This gifts me the permission to go forth without fear and on purpose.

I want to share with you a story about my younger sister (and biggest cheerleader), Emma Weaver. My sis has always been passionate about helping others, she has dedicated 26 of her 41 years to it. She is always giving, and showcasing others.

Then it happened, she felt the call to write her story. Step in big sis (me) with her super power of helping people write their stories by eliminating blocks, gifting tips and being efficient with time because let's face it, many of us are time poor!

Well, she did it, she wrote the book and brought it to a place where she could do no more so she handed it over to me and it was sent to my amazing editor, Dannielle. The synergy in that itself was amazing and I must share.

Emma's book was about IVF and her journey was woven

through the fictional story. Ultimately, she wrote the book she needed to read at the time. Dannielle had also been through IVF so connected deeply with the book and made it shine. I published the book, positioned my sister well in the market and we launched her. She became an international best-selling author overnight, was being called to do interviews and was on a huge trajectory aligned with her intention of building a mental wealth organisation from scratch. She was getting huge visibility and yet she didn't realise that this would happen by publishing her book. Ultimately, she had set a huge intention to build Mental Wealth International and unknowingly this book was a big part of that.

Do you see what happened here?

The thing that many people don't realise is that intentions are different from goals. Goals you plan, while with intentions you have to be prepared to action aligned opportunities even if you don't fully understand why at the time. The faith in your knowing will ensure your time is not wasted.

When we set an intention, an energetic ball is in motion. Things will shift around you and it's always a good idea to start shedding what no longer serves you so that you have the space in your life for what is to come.

It is important to set intentions because if you don't, you will never know what it is like to make possible what is perceived to be impossible. Now that's fun in motion!

When time and circumstance align, magic happens.

FIVE INTENTION
SETTING TECHNIQUES

There are many ways to manifest your intentions and it's important to know what works for you, what fits how you choose to produce the energy required for opportunities to find their way to you. Yes, they may be a little outside your comfort zone but you will easily identify them as stepping stones to the receipt of your intention, and this is where the magic happens.

I'm going to share five intention setting techniques that might appeal to you. Feel free to explore them yourself. I am all about channelling through my *Knowing* when it comes to my intentions but it can be fun to practise and see what you can make happen with the rest. You might find a practice that works wonders for you.

1. Use Your Imagination.

A concept I was introduced to recently and one that simplifies the act of attraction is called the 'pink bubble effect'. I really like it.

- Close your eyes and think about the one thing you wish you had.
- Keep your eyes closed and role play in your mind a scenario where you have it. Stay there for a moment.
- Now mentally grab a pink bubble and wrap it around your wish.
- Let it go knowing that it is now released and will come back to you at the perfect time.

The magic in this concept is in setting the intention, releasing it and Knowing when to connect and take action towards achieving it. When you set the intention, visualising the outcome and feeling that you have it right now starts the wheels in motion of manifesting the desire. Things will begin to shift around you to make room for what you requested.

* Shakti Gawain, an internationally renowned teacher of consciousness in her book, *Creative Visualization: Use the Power of Imagination to Create What You Want in Life.*

2. Vision Board

Collect imagery and write down words on a physical or electronic board to create a vision board. To have impact, it's good practice to have it somewhere you can see it every day and also feel what it is like to already have everything on it. Feel it to have it! You need to simply feel what it would be like to have those visions as a reality in your life.

I love vision boards, however I don't put all of my intentional focus onto them, instead I set intentions in motion and live aligned with them every day. For some people vision boards can have an adverse effect as their focus is so fixed on the end goal that they don't connect with the energy essence and so miss the stepping stone opportunities to get there. All they can think of is the end result so they miss the whole point of the journey to receiving.

I do, however, do an annual check-in vision board, especially for my writing. I have MANY book covers pinned to a corkboard for titles waiting to be written. My intention is to end up in a beautiful little house on a hill overlooking a forest with a bay window on the top floor and I write there every day for my readers, both non-fiction and fiction. A home where my grown up children (and their children) can come and go as they please, a home where everyone wants to come for Christmas Day. My heart is doing somersaults writing this.

3. Intention Journal

When you choose to set an intention, writing it down is setting it in motion. It is getting it out of your head and onto paper, initiating an action and therefore a commitment to the pursuit of that intention. As with any journal, you document your thoughts and the journey to receiving your intention. It is often the most magnificent thing to reflect on as you grow and a hugely valuable resource should you ever choose to write your story.

I created my own intention journal several years ago for a few reasons. Firstly, to jot down my intentions; secondly, to have a safe space to record the journey; and thirdly, I wrote 52 intention quotes (one for every week of the year) to inspire others to embrace their intentions.

4. Meditation

In order to connect with intentions that are aligned with our soul purpose, it is important to connect with the essence of who we are at the core. I am blessed with the natural ability of being able to do this due to a year-long inward journey in 2007 that I was guided into through my PTSD experience.

Meditation can be challenging for a busy mind, especially one that likes the busyness; but when you stop and clear the noise around you and in your mind, it is amazing what clarity and connection you can be gifted in this time.

I will never forget the time I went through a guided meditation and experienced excessive heart fluttering when the guide mentioned connecting with the true source of love within. I realised in that moment that the heart palpitations I had been experiencing were not a medical issue, they were in fact a physical reaction to the love of life I was experiencing at the time. Tears of relief trickled down my face. That might sound a little bizarre but the palpitations were so severe I had been put on a heart monitor to investigate the cause of them, but in fact it was my spiritual awakening in motion. This was during my time writing for *Building Beautiful Bonds* and *Universal Mind* magazine.

I now treat writing as my meditative state, a state of mind that I go into where I connect with a higher energy source and allow divine wisdom to flow through me.

Many people see meditation as unachievable because they struggle to silence their mind, but please know it is achievable and the more you do it without high expectations of yourself, the more of a natural process it becomes.

Do it your way and be open to progress so that you can advance your outcomes.

5. Plant an actual intention seed and nurture it to fruition

In this book I use the metaphor of an intention being a seed. Right now I am inviting you to plant an actual seed in the ground and nurture it to fruition. Put love into it and when you tend it, think of the intention you set aligned with that seed.

I planted a frangipani tree in front of my house. It is a tough, resilient tree and when it flowers it is beautiful. It is a representation of the empire I am growing. I nurture it and think positive thoughts when I tend to it. I pour love into it every day. I smile when I see it flower and know that even when it isn't looking so beautiful, there is magic happening on the inside to ensure that it flowers again.

Take a moment to think about a flower or plant that you would like to grow alongside your intention.

No matter how you choose to manifest your intentions it is important to know that unlike goals, an intention will reach its highest level of return when you embark on and embrace the journey. Try not to get distracted by unaligned opportunities that derail you, and the best way to do that is through KNOWING!

To recap on Knowing:

1. Feel it – When you set an intention, opportunities will come your way.
2. Think it – Ask yourself, 'Is this opportunity aligned with my intention?'
3. Action it – If the answer is *yes*, action it straight away; if it is *no* or *not sure*, then dismiss it.

I go in-depth into KNOWING in Book Two of this series, *The Power of Knowing,* where we learn the power in Knowing and how there is no fear in pursuing intentions through this source.

THE SEEDS OF INTENTION

'Intention is probably the most underrated and misunderstood phenomenon in terms of fulfilling potential and creating the life you want.'
Andrew Wallace - Intention

This is the first line in an extraordinary little book I discovered when I was researching intention.

One thing that stands out and that I could identify with, as a prolific seed scatterer, is that many of us do not take the time to test the soil in which our intention seeds are being planted. Look at a gardener for example, they make sure the seeds they are sowing are being planted in soil that will give them the best success rate to take root and blossom to their fullest potential. It is so important when setting intentions that we create a good environment for them to flourish.

We need to be aware of what energy we project onto our intention seeds. Studies have shown that plant seeds given love and spoken to flourished much faster and bloomed more successfully than those that were not. Imagine that, the energy of love and projecting human energy into an actual seed helped it to flourish. It is that type of energy fuel that our intention seedlings need.

How can you attract the opportunities you need that are aligned with your intention at the highest vibration if you are not at your highest vibration? The conditions in which you are planting your seed of intention will not sustain it. When you really nurture your seeds of intention with loving attention, they come to fruition a lot faster.

Sometimes seeds are nurtured for a time before they are planted into the soil and this gives them the best start to take root.

Take a moment to visualise this. The average person has more than 6000 thoughts each day. Imagine how many of them are intentions that we scattered aimlessly over the soil hoping they would take hold. Yet as soon as we walk away the scavenger birds are going to swoop down and gobble them up and maybe one lucky seed will find its way under the surface of the soil. Now visualise having a thought that you treasure, an intention seed that you really want to bring to fruition. You do a little bit of groundwork and help the seed take hold before going to your intention garden and planting it in nourished soil. Then you check in regularly to ensure the soil is kept nourished and the seed has the best chance of reaching the surface when you can watch it grow before your eyes, taking action when needed but witnessing the fruits of your labour blossom.

Those intentions are what life is all about, they make your heart sing, they are intentions that don't happen every day, they are big milestones in life and they are worth celebrating.

Be mindful that when you have an intention that you really want to happen, do the work at the start. Tap into your intuition of what that intention seed needs, do some research to give it the best chance and then when time and circumstance align, the magic will happen. You will be the one who benefits because you own the seed, you nurtured it to fruition and so you will reap the rewards.

INTENTIONS AND INSPIRED THOUGHTS

Intentions and inspired thoughts. What a powerful combination, I truly adore watching the process.

It can be misconceived that when we set an intention, we wait for an opportunity to present itself to us aligned with that intention, and that we just have to be aware that

1. The opportunity is aligned with our intention, and
2. That we have the courage to act straight away if it is.

That is not the only way to facilitate an intention.

Inspired thoughts are gifts from the universe that plant in our mind for a moment for us to action immediately because as quickly as they come into our mind, they can leave again. We are left with a residue of, *'What was that amazing thought I had, I wish I had written it down.'* Can you relate?

I have actioned and reaped the rewards of MANY inspired thoughts. I signed the Duchess of York to Serenity Press because of an inspired thought after setting an intention to make my publishing press more visible. The result is the most beautiful connection with the Duchess, a twenty-two-book deal, and our press was featured in hundreds of publications across the world.

Another time I set an intention to have Elizabeth Gilbert feature in one of my books, so I acted on an inspired thought, showed up at each step of the journey to it happening and made it easy for a yes decision.

One of the best pieces of advice I can give anyone about

actioning thoughts is that when you action a seedling of an idea, and you get a response, make it easy for the main people involved to say yes. Most people or businesses who have 'made it' need things to flow easily. Any sign of reluctance or a potential block might hinder a positive outcome.

And of course people who set intentions that are aligned with their values, which includes connecting with people of similar values, ensures that any outcome will feel worthwhile and without compromise.

Inspired thoughts come ready for you to act on them immediately! Please don't fall into the slippery slope of overthinking an inspired thought. You simply action it with your first impulse.

*We go inwards for the answer and outside for
the support to make it happen.*

Be confident in your inspired thoughts. Other people might not understand them and may even judge them as being unconventional, but leave that with them, don't take it on board, let the results speak for themselves. You are guaranteed results when you have the courage to act on inspired thoughts.

To conclude this chapter, inspired thoughts are gifts. They are gifts that bring you inward to think and subsequently action an interaction that will advance you towards your intentions.

THE JOURNEY AFTER SETTING AN INTENTION IS NOT YOURS TO CONTROL

In 2019 I set an intention to get my teeth fixed. My teeth never survived having six children and when pregnant with my fifth child five teeth shattered in my mouth. It had come to the point where I had no teeth at the two sides of my mouth, only stumps, and my front teeth were constantly moving. My mouth was so unhealthy and my breath smelled terrible. I would wake in the middle of the night with lots of blood in my mouth. I had toothaches so bad the pain went right up the side of my face and into my head.

As I set the intention to get my teeth sorted once and for all I was open to the opportunity to make that happen. I was told I was at a high risk of stroke because of how bad my teeth were and it was advised that I get them out and replaced. Having a young family, this was a wake-up call! There was also family history of strokes so I wasn't prepared to take any chances. My children needed me to be my best self for them.

I explored some avenues and had some work done but ultimately it was all leading back to the same scenario, one that I didn't enjoy the thought of but knew I would have to accept and endure. I was scheduled to have my teeth removed and replaced one month before I was due to co-host a huge corporate event in an Irish castle.

I will never forget the day of the procedure. I dropped my kids off at school and drove to the dentist. I had successfully put it out of my head until then. The reality hit while I was sitting in the waiting room but I was steadfast. I was scheduled to have the procedure done in stages but I'm so glad the dentist appreciated my personal situation and offered to do it all at once. My dentist was really amazing, he made me feel at ease and I am sure it was traumatic for him too, I could see it in his eyes when it was all over hours later. I did not feel any pain, I was awake the whole time. The biggest challenge was to keep my mind occupied, but I did and truly got to see my strength.

I was surprised that afterwards the pain was not as bad as I had expected. My mouth was sore and I couldn't take the high dose painkillers prescribed as I needed to be alert at all times for my children and also do school runs. But there was an aspect I wasn't prepared for and that was the grief I felt. I never expected it! It caught me off guard and sank me into sadness, real death sadness.

I needed to honour the process of physical healing and now also emotional healing. My kids were so beautiful, they took care of me and knew that Mummy wasn't feeling well. The thing about having lots of girls is that they love playing nurse. They kept my spirits up and with a trip home to Ireland to look forward to I had a deadline for when I wanted to feel better. It was the distraction I needed.

It was so worth it, as I feel healthier and I can now smile with pride. When I look back on the pictures from that trip I don't see sadness, I see a happy heart and a beautiful smile and I am grateful that I saw it through.

You see, one thing to be mindful of when setting intentions is that you will not know what you are signing up for beforehand. Yes, you are in the driving seat and call the shots but if you are truly dedicated to achieving the intention you set, the opportunities that present themselves to you may not be ideal yet are necessary.

Intentions are a commitment to an end result. Goals are planned, intentions are embraced.

THE IMPORTANCE OF
REGULAR DECLUTTERING

When we set an intention, things will start to shift around us for it to find its way to us and quite often we have to start a process of clearing because our lives are too full. You'll find things that no longer serve you start to fall away. If we don't allow those things to filter away, then we become overwhelmed because there's too much going on in our lives. Don't hoard life!

I know this because I have done this. I have kept taking on, taking on, taking on, without stopping to intentionally declutter my life from the debris of things that do not serve me anymore. I have discovered that it is a really good habit for me to do this regularly. It used to be every year, then reduced to six months, and is probably going to be every three months soon because things are moving at a faster pace.

When you build momentum, when you set big intentions in motion, when you're doing lots of things, it's important to keep decluttering as you go along. You don't want to hold onto stuff that doesn't serve you anymore because it wears you down and depletes your energy, and in order to keep achieving, you want to live at a high vibration and won't want anything to bring your frequency down. That is why it is super important to stop and declutter. It is good practice if with every intention you set, you let something go. That way you have the opportunity to choose instead of being forced to let go of something you want to hold onto.

It's so important because if you don't, you may get overwhelmed, you will be too far in and might even end up getting sick as a result of doing too much. You risk burnout.

Consider also that your rubbish may be somebody else's treasure. If there is something in your life that no longer serves you, pass it on or sell it to somebody else who will value it. I promise you, there will be somebody who will see value in it.

It's imperative that you step back and let go or create a divide there because you don't need that energy pulling you back, it doesn't serve you when you are setting intentions. To supercharge forward you need to get to the realm of a high vibrational energy field. So in that light, please honour that and undo the clutter as you go along.

When you start these amazing intentions, how is the magic of them supposed to shine into your life if everything is too full? Look at your life as a sphere around you and you are in there living your life. If your life is jam-packed, how can the magic shine in?

My four top tips for decluttering your life are:

1. Write a comprehensive list of EVERYTHING that takes up your time right now. (Work towards letting go of what no longer serves you on that list).
2. Consider where you are focusing your energy. Is it positive? Does it recharge you? Can you let go of some of that energy commitment now? Maybe give it less energy?
3. Remember to always keep your core values close to your heart and make all decisions through that funnel.
4. Remember some things and people are only in your life for a season, it does not serve you or them/it if you hold on for longer.

When you intentionally create the space and declutter to make room it will lighten you. You will feel instantly freer and may even decide not to fill up the space quite so much next time. If you're in business, delegating can be your best friend. For me and my business, growth happened when I learned how to delegate, which meant I could stay in my genius zone, doing what I love. Dream scenario right there! By mindfully setting an intention to create the space, things began to flow more naturally. I do the same when I am writing my books. I declutter to salvage the much-needed time to create and I also prioritise my writing. It is important to me to find time to write these books and share them with you, which means that I also must give myself permission to prioritise it as much as I would a business appointment. Even, for the period of time I am writing, I gift myself permission to not do so many extra family activities. My children are perfectly happy playing in our backyard, or using their imagination playing with their dolls' house, or even (my favourite) let them get bored because that is when creativity flourishes. I do adore those words, 'Mum, I'm bored.' I always offer to alleviate that boredom by finding them a chore to do. Funny how that initiates a creative mind.

You will get amazing results from decluttering but be mindful of your energy because some things we let go of need us to take a moment to honour them and maybe even grieve the loss. They will have served us and it is now time to move on so it is important to process and release any emotions connected to that. Don't just suppress the feelings, block them off and heartlessly move forward. Honour the feelings that come to the surface and allow the grief to pass through you so that you free yourself and don't have any residue lingering after you move on.

I know lots of people who volunteer their time and that is wonderful. I volunteer for lots of things, but everything I volunteer for serves me where I am at that period in my life and therefore it adds to my pot. When something begins to take away from my pot, then it is time to move on and let someone else have the opportunity to evolve through the opportunity. It doesn't serve you or them to hang on after it is time to go. Is there something you are doing right now that you can move on from?

SHARING YOUR INTENTIONS WITH THE RIGHT PEOPLE

However you choose to set your intentions, sharing them with the right people will ensure that you stay committed and maybe even get some support to make your dreams become reality.

Some of the people to share with are:
- Your cheerleaders
- The media
- Family who support your dreams
- Decision makers in the arena of your intentions
- Yourself on a regular basis.
- People who it is best not to share with:
- People who do not get it.
- Competitors
- Those jealous of others' success.

So why share your intentions at all?

There are pros and cons to sharing your intentions, especially in the early stages but I believe the pros outweigh the cons, so when an intention starts to take hold it is good to put it out there amongst the right people.

There have been times that I wished I had not shared but that was because I shared too early. I now know the right time to share is when the thought evolves in my mind. If I have a seedling of an idea, I give it time to germinate in my mind and if it is still there probing at me a few days later, well there is something in it.

Let those you love and spend the most time with understand

that your focus may be diverted because you have set an intention. When you have their support, it's great, when you don't it's not as easy but still not necessarily a block. I highly recommend only letting the positive, supportive energy in.

In my experience if you are upfront and say that whatever it is, is important to you then they will come round. Some people don't like the thought of something changing and so there might be some resistance but remember it is your intention, not theirs. My partner was not always supportive of my intentions, they were huge, and I understand how overwhelming that can be to load onto others who don't share the passion. But stick it out if it means a lot to you.

Sharing with the people who *get it* is a very important aspect, especially when you feel the urge to share with someone, and our intuition guides us to who to tell. Intentions are more powerful when you share them with people who can help make them real.

Some people may say you're procrastinating when you talk about an intention and it doesn't come to fruition straight away, but I don't believe that because it is not up to us to determine when the time and circumstance aligns for our dreams to become reality. We just need to keep showing up and not abandon the idea at the eleventh hour. I see too many dreams abandoned in what could be a moment before a breakthrough. The missing ingredient is faith. You are setting the scene and setting an intention that gathers the vibration and starts to become a reality.

The key ingredient here is that you must tell the right people.

If you are the type of personality (like me) who is stubborn and when people say that something isn't possible, it fuels the fire to go for it more, then you won't be daunted by the non-believers, the un-supporters, the people who use their energy to pull you down instead of using it to lift themselves up, so share away. They are equally important to your journey because we know that anything is possible when we put our minds to it!

So it's very important when you have the courage to share an intention in the world that you share with the right people so they add to your vibrational energy that goes into that intention so that it can reach far and wide. That vibrational energy is also actionable energy, because if they understand what it is that you're wanting to achieve, they may have the absolute desire to help you achieve it.

Good people do that. For example, I never anticipated that a conversation I had with someone would lead to my dream of being asked to speak on a TEDx stage. And when I chatted with him, I never expected him to ask me to be on his stage. But it happened through having the courage to share my intentions with the right people and by genuinely showing up, it led to a natural progression that flowed into a dream.

Share your intentions with *your* people, not just with anybody, and they will pick up momentum, they will expand vibrationally and energetically become a tangible product of your thoughts and actions. By owning the intention you are putting it out there. But put it out there with the right people so they can help you!

ACTING ON INTENTION

People who make it are not the overnight sensations we deem them to be, it takes a lot of navigating to position yourself for success. One true overnight success story I like to share is that of Spanx founder Sara Blakely. I absolutely get this woman. Her passion, focus, drive and most importantly, unwavering Knowing shines through. I recently watched an interview she did with Tony Robbins and to listen to her share every aspect of her journey to shine the light for others made my heart swell with delight.

The focus was not on her big breakthrough when Oprah brought her on the show. The focus was on how she navigated a breakthrough with getting her product into a chain of seven stores in the US. Sara didn't know how it was usually done eg via trade shows etc. Her instinct said to call and not leave a message, but to get someone on the other end in the buying department to answer and secure a 10-minute slot with them. She flew there and five minutes in she knew she was losing her buyer so she took action straight away and said, 'Can you come to the bathroom with me.' She used herself as a model to show her Spanx under white trousers and then also without them. The visual got her the deal, gave the buyer the impact they needed to say yes.

But let's talk about the idea and how it came to be in the first place. Sara was a salesperson for many years before the Spanx idea came to her. She describes a tear-filled desperate moment in which she felt like she was in the wrong movie, looked up to the universe and asked for an idea for her own product to sell. One day after cutting the legs out of some pantihose Sara realised that was her idea and so she ran with it.

After getting the seven stores on board she actually paid her friends to go in and buy the products. She also drove to every store during a 21-day road trip, spent the day there and got the staff excited about her product. Sara sold directly to customers and her bubbly nature was embraced on many levels. She got actionable! Even after being on Oprah's show, Sara has remained a close friend with her customers and is very proactive in her business.

We can learn so much from this story about the process of intention and I strongly recommend that you watch the interview. You will witness intention in action. Sara encompassed each one of the life principles I speak on in this series.

1. **Mindfulness:** She was mindful of the opportunities coming to her and mindful to take action.
2. **Knowing:** Listen to her story; you will know that she followed her Knowing!
3. **Intention:** She absolutely set a powerful intention and stuck to it.
4. **Gratitude:** She was so grateful for every opportunity and took nothing for granted. Gratitude is currency when it comes to opportunity.
5. **Love:** By goodness did she not (and still does) pursue this with loving intention!
6. **Forgiveness:** She held no grudges, she learned and moved on. This gifted her the freedom to move forward with nothing holding her back!
7. **Belief:** She absolutely believed in her product and herself because it wasn't about her, it was about helping women feel good, it became her mission.

I would like you to take a moment to think about how you do life. Is there something you can learn from Sara's story, or someone else who you look up to, that you can apply to your own life? Learn from people like Sara who takes ownership of her own life and goes for it. We can all get inspired by others but what we do with that inspiration, how we interpret that in our own lives to fuel our intentions is what will make us stand out from the crowd. Be inspired, be innovative, be open-minded.

FOCUS AND FAITH.
ARE YOU A BELIEVER?

Do you believe in the power of intention? It can be hard to believe in something if you can't see it with your eyes or feel it with your hands. Yet the most amazing things that have happened in my life come from having faith that all will turn out exactly as it is meant to, and that I will show up and go on the journey when needed to move things along.

I one hundred percent believe in the magic of intention. There is science in it but I love to think of the magic in it too.

One thing we do not want to do is feed into the cycle of overthinking as that often leads to analysis paralysis and that serves no one.

Had I overthought when I set the intention to write my first novel in 2010 it would not have happened and had that not happened, I would not have found my true calling and path into publishing. It does not bear thinking about!

But the seed was planted when a conversation I had with a friend gifted me the belief that writing a novel was possible. I had limiting beliefs around that, which I had to shatter. When I started to believe in the possibility, I also became more open minded and aware of the signs coming my way that led to writing my first book. Once that limiting belief was dispelled there was nothing holding me back. No excuses could be made, possibility grew into potential and subsequently a series of serendipitous events led to me sitting down at my computer on November 1st 2010 to write 1667 words a day for 30 days and produce a first draft of my first novel.

None of this would have been possible if I did not have faith in the outcome and believe that it was possible. And if I failed it was not the end of the world because at least I had tried.

So many people cannot see past their own limitations, quite often stemming from childhood. That is OK if those beliefs serve us as adults but when they don't, we need to do the work to unlearn them and release the control they have on our mind. When that happens in your life it changes you from the person you were before, to the person you now are. It is a truly instant and magical feeling. One to treasure!

There's nothing like that feeling of knowing when something is absolutely aligned and you get an inspired thought. You may have to have courage to action it but you have unwavering knowledge that it is aligned with the intention that you set. It's so important when the inspired thoughts or opportunities come to you that you have created the right vibrational frequency. It means that you can reach the highest heights with your intentions.

When time and circumstance align, that is when the magic happens. So set your intention, be patient, be aware, be focused and watch as the results come rolling in. Focus is a big thing with intention, and the belief we have in ourselves supports that.

Laser focus means that you are feeding into the frequency of that intention and inspired thoughts, opportunities and messages come to you quicker and easier when you believe with all of your heart.

ARE YOU AWARE OF THE POWER IN YOUR INTENTIONS?

One of the most under-rated powers that we all have instant access to is intention. I use it all the time to make huge things happen in my life. I have observed that the block for other people is the fear associated with setting a strong intention. I totally get that but it's important to remember that although an intention requires you to be all in with no guarantee on the outcome, you can still navigate the process without feeling like a failure. Quite often a failed intention shifts you on a path to a bigger and better intention. With that simple shift in perception you no longer need to feel like you are procrastinating in some way, because ultimately you are on a journey, or as I like to call it, an adventure.

To attract what is aligned for you, feel like you already have it, visualise it! However to receive it often requires us to become a higher version of ourselves because we are not fully ready when we set the intention. Powerful intentions are usually big dreams or goals and we have to embark on a journey of self-evolution. That means facing opportunities (challenges) to evolve. I have chatted about my perception of challenges in my other books but it is always worth repeating. Challenges are not brick walls, they are an opportunity to step up into the higher form of ourselves that we need to be to receive our heart's desires and achieve the goals we set. The bigger the goals, the bigger the steps! So yes, it takes courage to reach for the stars but goodness me, what an adventure it is.

Setting an intention energetically sets a powerful current in motion that will ripple to every atom in your body, emitting a force out into the universe that you are often unaware of at the time. That force penetrates the magnetic field and initiates a series of events that when you identify them as being connected to your intentions can lead to a realisation of just how powerful an influence you are on the experiences you have in this lifetime.

Some of the most powerful outcomes I have achieved in my life have been through setting powerful intentions and remaining aware enough to know that the journey to receiving those intentions is not mine to control, but it is mine to navigate. We are the navigators of our own destiny and you can either choose to identify that and have fun making awesome things happen in your life, or you can turn your back on it and never reach the highest version of yourself.

I will talk about aligned intentions versus ego-based endeavours because it is important to identify what is aligned with your highest potential and what is just a selfish pursuit that does not advance us in any way. I have done both many times and I have to say there is nothing like the feeling and rewards that come from being in total alignment with your highest potential. Many people do not get to experience that for themselves in their lifetime and that makes me very sad indeed. So ask yourself the question, 'Have I ever felt truly aligned?' I promise you that you will know if you have.

Setting clear intentions not only relieves us from the stress of uncertainty, it also gifts us focus and clarity.

The three steps of intention success.
1. Set the intention,
2. Connect with the knowing
3. Stay the course. When time and circumstance align, magic happens.

THE COLOSSAL POWER OF
A LOVING INTENTION

There is a power almighty, and it is closer to your grasp than you could ever imagine. It is simply loving intention!

I am living proof that when you pursue a thought and action it with loving intention you can make ANYTHING happen in your life.

A loving intention can heal the most broken bond, a body that needs regenerating and much more than we can fathom. Why? Because loving intention is the fuel of superheroes; it shines a light into any darkness. The evidence is there in your own life should you choose to see it.

Think about two people in your life who have faced similar challenges, be it health, financial, educational etc. Observe how one with loving support and positive healing intentions came through that challenge faster and healthier than someone with a negative mindset and outside influences. Now think about the person who didn't approach the challenge with self-love and had no support. Did they fall further into a downward spiral? Did they hit rock bottom before they rebuilt? Did they become even more unwell or take longer to heal? Or, have they let the challenge define them instead of empowering them?

There are so many different aspects that can be explored but one thing is certain: loving intention will always prevail.

I encourage us all to interact with loving intention when we can. It can ripple out and touch the lives of so many others. Let love prevail.

I will explore The Law of Love in Book Five of The Alchemy

of Life Magic series, but when writing on intention I cannot step around the power of this perfect duo because together they are a match made in Heaven!

When we take a moment to think on each individually, we see the potential. Combined, they are a powerful force in our lives and one I believe we have all felt at some time. So why do they work so well together?

The following from The Happiness Coach, Lori Brant captures it beautifully:

Bringing awareness to your state of BEing before you set your intentions allows you to align yourself with who you really are, fuel the intention with love and create more loving experiences in your life. There are two states of BEing, FEAR and LOVE. Remember, what you put out into the Universe comes back to you multiplied. Intentions set from a state of fear can create more fear compared to intentions that are set from a state of love, which can create more to love.

INTENTION AND FOCUS

There is infinite power in your intentions when you fuel them with focus. This is one of the keys to success! Whenever you are setting an intention, being aware and mindful of what you are giving energy to is very important. What you are thinking of the most is what you are going to attract the most and if you are lucky enough to live life on a high vibration then aligned opportunities will be lining up to present themselves to you. It's important to ensure that when you set the intention, all of your thoughts are positive and aligned with what you want to achieve. *Distracted thoughts get diverted results.*

So, let's explore focus for a moment. I believe there are various levels of focus.

1. **Absolute focus**
2. **Hopeful focus**
3. **Core Value focus**
4. **Distracted focus**

Let me share with you my definition of each.

- **Absolute focus** is when someone is all in and keeps their intentions close to their mind at all times, ready to pounce on an opportunity at any time. They may even compromise some of their values in the process because the hunger to achieve is so strong.

- **Hopeful focus** is when someone sets an intention but does not apply much focus to it, hoping that it will manifest itself. They hope that it will be handed to them on a plate.

- **Core Value focus** is my favourite. It is when someone sets an intention with absolute focus but aligns any decisions with their core values so that they do not jeopardise their happiness in the pursuit of their goals.

- **Distracted focus** is when someone thinks they want something but deep down they don't because their focus keeps navigating away from the intention they have set. If you have distracted focus when setting intentions, consider two things.

    1. Is it the right time for this intention to happen?
    2. Is this something that you think you want to achieve or something your heart is not in?

I can promise you that when something is truly aligned with your higher purpose you will not get distracted. It will make your heart beat that little bit faster, it will wake you up in the middle of the night with excitement and it will be the best adventure of your life.

I focus most intently when I am producing books. Each project will receive full focus to get it through production and over the line. It is when I don't stop and give full focus at the important times in the schedule that things go wrong. Things that matter to you deserve your full focus.

When I am focused on my personal intentions, I may have a different hat on but I have the same level of commitment. I make sure to check in and focus some high vibrational thoughts on my personal endeavours regularly because they are as important as my professional goals.

There are things that you can leave to the universe that will align when the time is right, but there's a lot of background work that has to happen as well and understanding that is important. Focus will be required so be prepared for that because that's what we sign up to when we set powerful intentions.

It's work that is making something magnificent happen, so that is why focus is important. Your focus will be rewarded, your hard work will be rewarded when it's aligned with your intentions, and you know that because you feel that energetically within yourself. It's actually science! Think about your energy, your atoms, your body, the biology of you and feel that deeply because we're all one, tapped into an electrical current; you will know it and feel it.

If it's energetically aligned with what you're pursuing it will light you up; if it's not, then it's just going to feel like a slug because, you know, that has you going nowhere.

Focus and set the goals and enjoy the journey of making it all come together.

What type of focus will you give your intentions?

INTENTION AND CASH FLOW

I believe we all have lessons to learn when it comes to money. It is one of the things I feel is valued way too much in this world when time and even kindness are worth more. I know money can make wonderful things happen in the world but my issue is that the wrong types of people are prioritising money. We need more good people prioritising money in their lives because when good people have money, good things happen!

One of my life lessons is about money. I am an in-one-hand-out-the-other type of person. (Anyone relate?) I set an intention for a million dollar year, and I achieved it. Yes, I made a million dollars in one year, but I also spent one million dollars. Why? Because I see money as potential for growth. If there was a value on the experiences, things I have made happen with that money, then I would be a billionaire. I use money to fuel bigger intentions and sometimes that means waiting. Patience is a virtue I have come to value immensely.

Yes, I may have a forward thinking attitude to money but I am also a good person and through the money I earn, jobs are created, books and stories are shared with the world and I am building the wealth of a press that will hopefully sustain me in my latter years.

Where there is a will there is always a way is one of my life mottos and so when I set an intention and want it enough, then the money needed comes flooding in because I believe it will and I never have any fear around money. Money is a commodity to make things happen, to keep my family living a beautiful life, to give to others so that life can be better for them. Money is good as it can do good things.

Think about your relationship with money. How do you feel about it? Are you in a scarcity or abundant mindset the majority of the time?

Our attitude to money at any given time is reflected in our daily lives and our dominant thoughts.

There are times when I feel like the richest person and there are other times when I am robbing Peter to pay Paul. I don't know if I will ever be different and I don't know if I ever want to be. It makes me feel alive. When I need to manifest money it is a hunger to make something wonderful happen and motivates me to get up and provide value to others so that I can achieve wonderful things for myself and them. Everything I do is through honest to goodness intention to do goodness. And that, I have found, is always rewarded.

One of the biggest lessons we can learn from money is that if we have an abundant mindset when it comes to outgoings and a scarcity mindset when it comes to income then we need to be mindful of that. The person who gives a lot financially will need to fill up the cash reserves. I'm a giver and creator so I struggle with this in the sense of I know what to do and have done it, but enjoy more the creating things from money part more than the saving part. It's kind of like the saying that the money burns a hole in my pocket. I do know that if I won Lotto I would give most of it away, not recklessly but to share more goodness with the world through programs, free resources etc. I would give my most precious commodity of time to others.

One of the elements of money I struggle with is who determines what good practice is when it comes to finances. People say that money makes the world go around, I say love makes the world go around.

I love what money can make happen in my life and in the lives of others. I also realise how lack of money mindset or recklessness through gambling etc can ruin and consume someone's life.

Money is energy so it is important to know what it is for you. What is your money story? Do you host limiting beliefs from your childhood that don't serve you now? Most of us do and that's OK but we can unlearn things in our adulthood and create our own personalised belief system that will serve us better and fuel our dreams.

There is no reason why you can't be the next person to win Lotto. Do you believe you can? Do you even do Lotto? It's all an energy exchange. I often say to the Lotto person, '*I'm going to come in here one day, scan my ticket and the machine will say, your ticket is a winner, would you like to know the amount? And when I click yes it will have a six figure sum there.*' I believe that I have as good a chance as anyone and my part in the energy exchange is to show up, choose my numbers and buy my ticket. Whether the lady behind the counter believes me or not is irrelevant; what is relevant is that I believe it.

One thing I know for sure is that when you think at a higher vibration money flows more easily. I have used *The Secret Money app* to shift my mindset to abundant thinking. The affirmations help eliminate negative money thoughts and I recommend it. Money is energy. When you come to realise this it may overwhelm you at first but once you play around with it and get some traction when you focus on positive money thoughts and frequency, then you will see a dramatic change in your bank balance.

It's important to remember that as money is energy it does require energy to generate it. Be mindful of how much time and what you are willing to compromise to manifest this into your life. It may not be an energy or a side of you that people who love you like to experience. But it is important to remember that to do good things in the world money helps immensely. For example, I used to be able to sustain my life at a much lower cost but as I have raised my vibration and the things I want to achieve then I needed to align with that and raise the cash flow to sustain it. I've had a huge evolutionary process, so much so that in the past five years, my income has increased to ten times what it was to keep my businesses going, which is wonderful.

I'm able to have staff and do all of those high level things I want to do. To sustain that business, every now and again I need to stop relying on my intentions and build up the cash flow bank. When that happens, I go back into doing the work that sustains the business. It is a cycle that I've come to identify and embrace and I use it to align with my values and ensure that I have a work/life balance because that is so important to me.

And of course, this does not just apply to business, it also applies to life. If you want to manifest a holiday, set the intention and work with what that is for you, feel what it is like and be aware of opportunities to make it happen. It might not even be cash, it could be a competition. The main thing is to be aware that when you set the intention, it is in motion so don't block it from coming to you. Your job is to action the thoughts and opportunities that come your way.

My recommendation is if you want something in your life to change, you have to do things differently. Change an aspect of how you are doing something, change perspective.

We all know that when we act instead of react it sets a ball in motion and that is what we want. Super charge your abundant mindset through positive affirmations and maintain a high vibrational thought frequency when you think money!

What are your money ambitions? Do you believe they are achievable? Write down your money intentions for the next year, five years, ten years below.

UNIVERSAL THINKING
AND INTENTIONS

I was recently gifted the absolute gift of reading *The Universal One* written by Walter Russell. It is complex but I got the essence of it and understood the intricacies of this book that I believe was a game changer when it was released more than 100 years ago. Although quite philosophical, it is all about the oneness of thoughts and matter and how our thoughts create things. I adore this book, the language and deep level thoughts fascinate me. It was a gift from my dear friend and fellow quantum thinker Adrea L Peters, who knew I would 'get it'.

Walter talks of the one God, the Universal One, and how God is in everything we see and do and is in us also. God is omnipresent! I am talking about the almighty creator who we see as larger than anything but yet can be as small as anything too. Our thoughts create things, our thoughts are part of the omnipresence of God. When we realise that we have access to infinite power closer than we can ever imagine it begins to sink in that when we adjust to universal thinking we can change our reality with a mere thought.

So, let's make this relative to our daily lives. Taking responsibility that our thoughts create things is a pretty big responsibility. I know I have felt it. One thing I have come to realise is that many people pass the responsibility to others, therefore they pass the power over their lives to someone else too. How are we to reach our full potential if we pass the baton to someone else? They are not inside us, they don't know what makes us who we are, or what our soul needs. Only we as individuals will receive that magnificent feeling of knowing that we are on the right track, those beautiful serendipitous moments that come like little sign posts on our journey. For me they are the number 22. It pops up in front of me when I least expect it. Only yesterday I went to an adventure playground with my kids and out of a full box of numbers I could have been given out pops #22. I am mindful of that and it makes me smile every time I see this number. That smile and little glow is universal, it emits from my heart and becomes something lovely.

That is why we need to understand how significant universal thinking is when it comes to intentions. When we set an intention, it is in a process of becoming matter. Thoughts become things! It is a universal law. As philosopher Bob Proctor is well known for saying, *'If you can think it in your mind, you can feel it in your hand.'*

That goes for all thoughts and that is why I encourage everyone to maintain a positive thought vibration as often as possible because thoughts do become things and the universal law does not determine between positive or negative, it provides for all equally.

There are so many intricacies in life, the universe is in harmony with all, everything that we can feel, think and see. The following flowed from me after listening to Jo Dispenza have a conversation about how energy becomes matter. I was not going to keep it in the book but something called for it to stay and so here you go.

This universal law of motion is one of equilibrium from the beginning of a motion to the maximum potential of that motion. During its progression the stability exchanges, and its reality becomes an illusion of stability but is anything ever truly stable? There is a true position for every potential and when that is achieved maximum impact is made. The true position must be found for the exact dimensions of the universe or constant energy which is stored up as mass.

Have you ever thought about how you can really like something and for someone else it will just go over their head? They have no interest whereas to you it is an all-consuming passion. Think of it in terms of setting an intention; their intentions may not be super ambitious whereas yours are. What you pursue lights you up, fuels you and propels you forward and that is all that matters.

A quote you have probably heard me mention on a few occasions is, 'When time and circumstance align, magic happens.' What it means is, do what you can now with what you have and when the time and circumstances align then that is when you will reap the rewards. Patience is gruelling for ambitious people who want everything yesterday.

Whilst writing this paragraph something profound happened to me and it is all aligned with universal thinking and intentions as it was a sign that came after an inspired thought that I am to action. I was driving to Bunbury, south of Perth in Western Australia with my kids at approximately 7am. It is an hour and a half drive on the highway from our home and we were about half-way there. Suddenly I had a very clear inspired thought and a scenario played out in my mind. A thought popped into my head that I should go on my Facebook page to ask if any of my contacts could put me in touch with Oprah or her team. I then had a clear vision of me chatting with her first on a Zoom call and then in a Soul Sunday scenario. It was so clear, so comfortable and I knew it would happen and I would know when it was time.

The message was that we would chat about focus and faith and how it can get us to where we want in life. 'Full focus and Unwavering Faith'. It was one of those magical thoughts that I have had happen and have actioned in my life for magical results. But something next level happened, for a huge eagle flew in front of my windscreen, a couple of feet from my car. Its wings were spread wide, it looked exactly like the image below. For it to happen after my epiphany moment I knew it was a clear sign. So, when I got home, I googled the meaning of seeing a wedge-tailed eagle...

'Universally, eagles are a symbol of power; they can rise over the *world, seeing and understanding all. Possessing keen eyesight, they can have a higher perspective on things. They bypass "not seeing the forest for the trees" and can indicate a talent for problem-solving. If a Wedge-tailed Eagle crosses your path in flight, remember the ability you have in being able to take flight and view your world from a higher perspective, to see the bigger picture. An eagle can see the smallest movement and act quickly. You too can act as soon as you see your goal – don't wait, or your chance, like a startled rabbit, may be gone!'*

It blew my mind! Watch this space.

Intend things with passion, intend things with belief, intend things with vision greater than your thinking mind can ever imagine; give it permission to grow into what it needs to become in order for it to be worthy of your intention.

THE MIRACULOUS
HEALING THROUGH
COLLECTIVE INTENTIONS

I want to talk about miracles and the power of collective intentions to make miraculous things happen. Intentions can be set for our wealth, our goals, for all manner of things, but I want to touch on health because ultimately our health is our wealth. Without our health and the health of our family things don't flow. It is hard to get into that energy field of flow where everything just happens when health worries are foremost in our mind.

That brings me to the power of a collective.

I wrote about this in one of my novels, *The Wish Giver,* which featured the host of a circle who brought people together to generate energy to send that collective vibration to someone in a distant location who was in need of healing. The collective healing power was so powerful that it could be felt by the recipient. Yes, I do know that this is really hard for scientists to prove, but you cannot question the results. That's where the miracle in collective intention really demonstrates the intensity of the energy created and the potential that can be achieved through it. So why not embrace the miracle? Why question it when the results are what we want to achieve, especially when improved health is involved?

So let's go with the flow of it and embrace it and not question it. Just have faith in the collective healing power and don't fear an outcome that should instead be celebrated and embraced. It does require that we step beyond ourselves into that quantum realm, that field of energy where anything is possible, including miraculous healing.

The wonderful Lynne McTaggart, author of *The Intention Experiment*, has brought many, many people together online to heal people and recorded the results.

She has proven that when people come together in a collective energy and focus that energy on one specific thought, person or event something that can't be ignored happens. The frequency can actually be picked up on radars. When people come together who are in that quantum field and their attention on their emotions is absolutely aligned then high vibrational miracles happen. It can also happen individually but collectively the vibration can be picked up.

Collectively, that power is miraculous, it is what can happen because as Einstein taught us, the energy field influences matter. Sickness is matter; it's matter that is within our bodies. It's in the genetics of our bodies and our biology can shift when we focus energy from a healing field to that source and the proof is there. When many people combine their energies together and send it to that source a miracle can happen.

Why do so many people choose not to believe that? In doing that they can block the potential. Why go against that? Why not believe that those miracles happen? There's nothing to lose, only something to gain. I have faith that that is exactly what is happening through that energy, through that high vibrational field beyond ourselves, around where people meet collectively and have a combined energy field. I'm not almighty but I choose to do my bit.

Powerful energy field projects onto matter, onto illness, a cancer or an ailment, a broken heart, anything. When that occurs, miracles happen. Things start to shift within the universe to make things happen. So collectively, we need to think about what we can do within ourselves. What can we make happen collectively that will make miracles happen in our own lives, but also in other people's lives, because that's what will heal our world, that's what will heal our families, and that's what will make a real difference in our world.

I know it may seem intense, but my goodness, if we only knew the power that we have at our disposal the world would be a different place. When we let someone else lead the way we surrender our power instead of standing alongside them to make a difference. We may have different things that are important to us but I'm sure there are plenty of people who have the same interests, passions and values as you that you can connect with and create a super energy that is almighty, powerful and fuelled through love. That is the almightiest power of all because love conquers all. Have you ever felt what it is like to heal something through love? Maybe you haven't been mindful of it but most people heal through opening their hearts to others. In my next book in the series, *The Law of Love*, you learn all about the love and it is an almighty power.

But for now, let's focus on the miracle of the intentions that we can set to make our world and the world as a whole a better place. And can you imagine not giving back, for when you give you ultimately receive. It's not about karma, it's based on science and physics. You receive because you are in the energy of giving, and that energy and the miracles that you are projecting on other people is around you. You are going to benefit from that energetically, but also materially in the reality around you.

How exciting is that! Do we not all want more of that in our lives? I say *yes*. I say *yes* to miracles. I say *yes* to intentions. And I say *yes* to us making a difference in the health and wellbeing of others.

THE SHIFT IN ENERGY WHEN YOU LIVE THROUGH INTENTION

When you live through intention the impact on your life is instant. It does not take long to see things start to shift and align. Not all of it is wonderful but I cannot emphasise enough how important it is to focus on the positive opportunities and inspired thoughts that are being gifted to you.

It is a good time to mention that when we set intentions, the things in our lives that no longer serve us will start to fall away. It's all the ebb and flow of manifesting. We cannot hoard everything, in fact if you are reader of all of my books or part of my social platforms you will hear me talk on the importance of doing a life de-clutter every now and again. For me it is a small de-clutter every three months and a larger cull every year, usually when my children have summer holidays. Working with their calendar works for me because my life by design ensures that I adjust my pace at the end of every school term for two weeks and then a six-week slow down mainly in January. I urge you to find a similar flow that works in your life and just roll with it, committed but not painfully.

People in your world will align with your intentions just as you will align with theirs. To have support around you allows you to maintain magnificence.

Belief is an important principle when it comes to intentions because when you believe that something is possible it energises it, it lifts your energy and you will be present in a higher energy. I always suggest that you take a moment to have faith in the outcome even if you cannot see it right now. Trust that everything is conspiring to bring your intention from a thought vibration into a real life experience.

It is good to be mindful of your energy throughout the manifesting process but also allow it to flow and be exactly what it needs to be. Loving intention is usually a big part of everyone's intentions. If someone wants to manifest a lot of money, they must first believe it is possible and also love the feeling money brings to them. Being mindful of your energy and emotional levels benefits the process immensely. It is when I catch up on sleep, eat well and am happier in my day-to-day life that things flow and my intentions gain traction. This observation is personal, but I do believe it is universal because when we focus on reenergising our body and mind everyone and everything benefits.

So when you set intentions, know the power of your energy and be mindful to keep your mind, body and soul at its highest level of wellness so that your energy can do its job in making your heart's desires become your reality.

The Law
of Love

" *Love is the most powerful force in the universe; it is the only frequency that can transcend all time and space. It's literally all around us like oxygen.*"

BOB PROCTOR

MY LOVE PHILOSOPHY

When I think about love I think more than an intimate relationship with my partner I see a powerful pure energy that when channelled towards something will make it manifest to it highest potential. It's simple to navigate in theory but in practice it can get complicated.

- If you want a great relationship channel love into it,
- If you want more money, love money so much and don't feel shameful about it.
- If you want success in your business channel loving energy into every interaction you make
- If you want connection with your children, love then unconditionally not materialistically.
- If you want magic to happen in your life, believe in infinite possibilities with all of your heart.

These are a few examples of how to navigate love in our lives, you can easily add to this list. They may seem like simple statements, don't they? Yet we make it so complicated in practice. Love is all powerful, it is the divine energy that governs all of the laws, when navigated well it can make all of your heart's desires come to fruition and in turn love will ripple out to those around you and beyond. It can transcend oceans and quantum fields, love is almighty. You will hear me mention this many times in this book, that is because I want it to embed into your heart and mind because in the words of John Lennon, all we need is love, love is all we need!

Your love equation:
open heart + emotional flow + focused energy
= highest potential

Love is such an important principle. One that as humans we often neglect, abuse, or take for granted. Love is supposed to be simple. We just make it complicated because it often originates in our heart and our emotions can run high with it. Yet if we knew that we could leverage our emotions to supercharge our results we would put more effort into this universal governance.

I called this book The Law of Love because I know that entwined through all the universal laws that govern our lives (knowingly or unknowingly) Love is there fuelling everything should we choose it helping us find our way to the best results. Choose love always.

WHAT DOES LOVE MEAN TO YOU?

It's really important to recognise what your definition of love is. Think about how you perceive it now and compare that to how you see it when you finish reading this book.

It will help you to connect with the essence of the energy of love and it will also gift you faster access to it when you want to apply it to a scenario in your life.

Whether it be romantic or practical, your definition of love is personal and is always right, just for you.

My definition of love before reading this book is:

My definition of love after reading this book is:

THE LAW OF LOVE

Understanding that love is the purest form of energy and a power that we all have the instant ability to access can be a bit overwhelming for some people. I've talked many times about it being an infinite well that we can access at any time, and it is! We often get hurt in life and shield ourselves from love when in fact it is in those moments that we need to bask more in it. Some people unconsciously lock it away because of fear due to the things that have happened in their past and their vulnerability when they open up their hearts and share love.

We're all gifted that infinite supply of love should we choose to embrace it. But what are we to do with that infinite well of love?

We will all experience challenges in life and that means we are evolving. We will all have life lessons to endure that will sink our heart to the pit of our stomach and we may feel like we will never recover, but guess what, you will! When we fuel loving energy into the harsh moments just as we do into the exciting success-driven ones, then we will feel nurtured through every occurrence we endure in life.

Here I share something from Wikipedia because the "pure energy" it talks about is Love. It is an interesting perspective that love and the Universal laws are largely based on the user having faith in the practice, and yet the results far outweigh any questions asked.

*In the New Thought spiritual movement, the **Law of Attraction** is a pseudoscience based on the belief that positive or negative thoughts bring positive or negative experiences into a person's life. The belief is based on the ideas that people and their thoughts are made from* *"pure energy" and that a process of like energy attracting like energy exists through which a person can improve their health, wealth, and personal relationships. ...***Wikipedia**

Loving energy works in the way we want it to; it is there to serve us, so when we learn how to use it properly we will create one of the most impactful habits that will hold us in good stead for a lifetime. And the great thing is, there is a never-ending supply so you can share love freely in the knowledge that it will never dry up.

We must understand deeply that we must serve ourselves first and others after. When we serve ourselves first it means that others will get the best of us. Let me emphasise that. We are not here to sacrifice all of ourselves. We are here on this world to actually experience joy and through that joy to show up on life and have the best lives possible.

To truly work in alignment with the Law of Love we must choose love first! It must be our first response to everything, even the negative things because those scenarios are more in need of love than others.

We're not here to suffer. Contrary to everybody's belief, we can have our best lives possible if we choose to do so. So why suffer? Why, oh why is sacrifice put on a pedestal? We're not here to sacrifice ourselves. We are here to love ourselves and love one another and we can. That's what brings goodness into the world. When we serve ourselves first, we don't have any scarcity. We don't have any fears of lack. We only have love and quite often that is more than enough.

Choose love always!

WHY LOVE?

When we learn how to open our heart and love with all of ourself, we can make anything happen. Loving energy is the most powerful energy of all; it heals, it grows, it radiates through us and from us and when we choose love instead of fear, that is when the true magic of life can be experienced.

Connect with the love within exercise:

Did you know that love is an actual physical thing that you can gauge? You can identify when absolute divine love is flowing through you as it will feel like a physical surge through your heart. If you haven't connected to it as source energy the best way to do so is through a meditation.

When you learn how to connect with the loving energy source within you it will become more and more accessible when you are manifesting.

Loving energy is a super fuel when it comes to manifesting our desires.

1. Find a place where you feel peace.
2. Take a quiet moment and close your eyes.
3. Allow your mind time to settle and focus in on your heart organ.
4. Listen to the loving energy meditation or follow these words:

Your mind is an explorer on a quest to find the epitome of a pure loving energy source deep within you. It starts at your toes. Hold it there for a moment and feel how it glows right at the centre of your toe. It then slowly makes its way into your foot and begins to navigate through your body. It feels like a warm glow traveling through you. You can feel it deep at the centre of your being as it continues to travel past your ankle and up your leg right past your knee and slowly makes its way up to your groin, through your pelvic area and holds space in your tummy area, where you process nourishment. You feel full. And then it happens, it moves a little more upwards and lands in your heart. You feel its warmth as it surges through your heart with palpitations to let you know it beats only for you. Feel deeply as those palpations surge love through your veins. Know in this moment what it is like to feel divine love. The divine love that is always stored deep within you and that you can access any time. Know the power of this divine energy and how it can change any negative to a positive. Loving energy conquers all. Use it for your soul's purpose. Sit still in that energy for a moment and when you are ready, let your love seed travel up through your chest area, igniting you as it flows through to your throat where love- filled words will flow through, and up through your head to your mind where it has now created a special compartment for you to store and access this loving energy when you so wish. Loving energy is limitless, there is no end, the more you use the more it creates, it is infinite and so are you. Know your power and the power of the love within you.

5. Once you have harnessed the divine loving energy within you, you will be able to access it when you need to, to super charge any endeavour or connection.
6. Know that when you do something with loving intention you have given your best to any scenario and so you can show up authentically you.

Let everything you do be done through love.

SENDING LOVE AHEAD

Sending love ahead. Think about it for a moment. It's such a simple concept and yet so many people don't do it. Then there are others who do it without even realising it. I have lots of examples to share with you from my own personal endeavours. I could do it so much more than I do.

When you set the intention in it, it's much more powerful and when you do it constantly and consistently, it becomes part of your DNA. So learn to do it and wait till you see the results. You will live a more harmonious life, a life filled with loving responses when you send love ahead. For example, if you're going for a big job, or if you set an intention and you've acted on an inspired thought, or if you've had an argument with a loved one and you really want your next interaction to be more amicable.

There were times when I had an argument with my husband and he would go to work and yes, he would have time to stew on it and he believed that he was right. I would hold the anger, the frustration and the stubbornness within me towards our argument because I believed that I was right. Both of us were so passionate about our stances and not meeting in the middle to find a level playing field.

The energy within both of us was so powerful that you could actually feel it, even though he was 100 kilometres away and had a job. Then one day I when I started awakening, I thought, I'm going to try something and see if it works. I never told him or anybody else. I think I was pregnant at the time.

I thought, *OK, I know I want to be right. I know this is really important to me, but obviously there's something within him that's very important to him. So I'm willing to explore a solution together. I* sent love ahead and it was a different person who came home from work that day after what may have been days of not speaking to each other. It was amazing.

And yes, maybe my demeanour had changed and I understand that. But I honestly know that sending love ahead helped the situation 100 percent. In another example, I set an intention that I really wanted to get my books into the US and I had an inspired thought that I actioned. I sent books to a big publisher. Big risk, you know, big thing, so I sent them with love.

When I knew they had arrived, I followed up with an email and introduced myself, saying I knew it was a bit cheeky to do so. I got a really awesome reply, because in my emails I send love through them to the receiver and they can feel that, without a doubt. I'm sending love ahead and the replies I get are more connected.

Sending love works. So how do we do it? What are the strategies? One, you sit in the scenario, whether it be something you want to achieve or something you want to heal. Whatever it is, you sit in the energy of the ideal scenario of that. It is really powerful and really important that you sit in the energy of it and send love into it.

You will see the results and whatever you might think, there's no questioning results. I don't overthink it. I just embrace it. It works. You can actually physically heal someone by sending love ahead and this is especially powerful when people come together in a collective to send loving, healing energy to a source of ill health.

Self-help author and lecturer Bob Proctor teaches that diseases and ill health are when your body is not at ease. When we send love ahead, that's right at a target. Whether it be a country, a town or an individual, they all receive that energy because energy can be like a sonic boom. It propels across many, many miles to reach where it needs to go, because when you target energy at a single source, it receives it.

Similar to the way we can contact someone by phone on the other side of the world in an instant, we humans are energy transmitters. Whenever we target something or someone and send love, it will be received. It is all the more powerful when the receiver knows it's coming because they're open to receiving the transmission but it doesn't have to necessarily be that way.

Try the concept of the three-step strategy. One, sit in the energy. Sit in the moment to connect with your heart centre. You can use the loving energy meditation I shared to really connect with your heart centre where you can compile a ball of that loving essence. You know how powerful that energy is and you can project it to where it is needed. Remember, it's not as if it's going to dry up.

The more you use it, the more you're going to have. OK, you can use it on others, on yourself, on a scenario, but whatever it is, just use it for good because love conquers all. Love is all. God is love. We are love. The more we embrace love, the more goodness we and others can experience. The third step of that process after you compile the love is to really target it, to send it where it needs to go. Feel the love with all your heart and just catapult it to where it needs to go, and smile.

Be grateful that you have that love to give. Please know that you are so powerful, more powerful than you can ever know. I have done this and if I can do it, you can do it. We all have the same abilities and we just need to access them. When you learn how to unlock your infinite well of love, anything can happen. Enjoy!

UNCONDITIONAL LOVE

One thing I can say for certain is that love has played a big part in my life. I have been blessed enough to know unconditional love from the day I was born. If you are reading this and don't have a foundation of unconditional love from your childhood, don't worry. It might take a little effort but you will be able to capture and apply it to your future from now. It can become a habit from any age, as it's a choice to behold the mindful practice of identifying when you have experienced unconditional love in your life and treasure each moment of it.

I know that I was born from that beautiful connection between two people who so wanted a child to love. That is one of the most beautiful essences to be borne from and I do feel truly blessed. True, such love, they never take it for granted.

Have you ever thought about the essence of the love that you were borne from? I remember my sister talking about her IVF journey. She had been through three IVF journeys and on her third one, she knew it was going to be successful because when the embryo was implanted, she saw a light flash. She knew in that moment. I get goose bumps every time I think of it. True pure life. Implanted and getting ready to be born. Oh, it just gives me shivers.

As much as loving, intimate connections with our family, our partners and our children is important, the energy of love is forever flowing through us, around us, and entangling in every aspect of our lives. Loving energy is so much more than an interaction between two people. It is an absolutely amazing relationship with the whole of humanity and the universe. When we are opened and we live through love, where we choose to see the best in people, when we choose to show off the best of ourselves and do the work that we need to do in ourselves so that we can be the best for others, it is so powerful.

It is so powerful that you cannot mistake it for anything else, you just feel it. There's nothing like the feeling of true love. Love for yourself. Love for your life. Love for others. Because through that love, you always want the best. You always want the best outcome for everyone involved, not just for yourself. You don't live life as a selfish endeavour, you live life with the best outcome in mind, not just for you, but for everyone.

That is how the law works. We need more people living through the law of love. We need more people honouring love, not fearing it. So many people fear love yet love is to be embraced, love is to be shared, love is to be celebrated because love conquers all. It allows us to grow, to heal, to evolve, to connect, to make this world a better place for now and for future generations.

It is the most important aspect of all humanity. We need to learn how to love, how to love with an open heart, not just how to love with one person. We need to open our minds when it comes to love, because when we do, we change things, we change people, we change our world. We make amazing things happen. Miracles happen because of love, love, love. It needs to be embraced because it makes the world a better place.

CONNECTING TO DIVINE
LOVE SOURCE EXERCISE

To connect to love you will need to find stillness. In this busy bee world we now live in, it can be tough to access love straight away. If you do not already have an automatic tendency to go to love when acting or reacting then you will need to rewire your heart and mind.

It will be tougher for some people than others. I highly recommend that you visit the work of Louise Hay or other wonderful love motivated philosophers so that you can get into the headspace of connecting to that energy. It will open your mind to the possibility and make it easier for you to tap into it.

Please know that you might start to have a physical response to this. I did when I reconnected.

I have shared in the past that I thought that there was something wrong with my heart because I was experiencing erratic heart flutters. They scared me, and I even ended up on a heart monitor. I was very much a mum at home all of the time and quite out of the blue a friend asked me if I would like to join her for a meditation at another woman's home nearby. It was quite intimate, just four of us, and I had never meditated before so it was new to me. I just knew that something was calling me. Little did I know that I was to experience a moment that would change my life.

We relaxed into our chairs and the lady played a meditation tape which featured the voice of a man from an eastern culture. It was quite off-putting at first but I rolled with it. It took a few minutes but I relaxed into it as he led us through focal points in our body, first starting at our toes and moving upwards. When he came to our heart, he spoke about feeling the love our heart has in abundance and how we can break the layer we have covered it in, allowing it to shatter so that we can love freely, and through love everything grows. Well, in that very moment my heart fluttered so much that my cheeks flushed, and I identified it to be the same heart flutter that had been concerning me enough to go to my doctor who had put me on a heart monitor for a day. The realisation that I ignited this reaction changed me. Tears of relief streamed down my cheeks and I knew that my heart flutters were nothing to fear. They were in fact something to embrace and action, something that I could use to grow the love in my life, and at that time it was self-love I needed most as I was pouring so much into my beautiful family but not myself. It had never occurred to me that you can't pour from an empty cup and from then on, I ensured that I took time to refill my cup. Going to this meditation itself was pouring into my cup as I had a six-week-old who I would never have left for a moment before; and you know what, she survived and we had more fulfilling hugs on my return.

One other thing happened that night that I must share before I finish this story. At first when we came out of the meditation, I said nothing but the group had felt the pulsating energy radiating from me so I told them about my self-discovery. We then went on to tap into a message for each other my immediate thought was *Oh no, I'm not going to be able to do this*, but I tried. When I tapped into the energy of the lady I was to get a message for, my ear began hurting badly with a sharp stabbing pain that was so distinct I couldn't ignore it, and a message came through that healing was in motion. I relayed what I felt and thought and it turned out her grandson was experiencing really bad ear infections and they were all worried.

I share the latter because when messages come through us for others it can really help so we should not keep them to ourselves. We just share and let them do what is needed with the message. That too is love in motion and can make a huge difference. I have on many occasions activated an inspired thought that has come into my heart and mind for someone, and I share without worrying that they might think I am crazy. It may not make sense in that moment but it will later on to them, and I often get a message back saying, "Remember you told me this, well…" Yes, that takes courage and for inhibitions to be in check.

So how will you tap into your divine love source? Follow the steps on the next page to help you ignite your divine love source and it will become increasingly easier to access it.

STEP 1

Expose yourself to a loving
energy source higher than
you normally experience by
listening to someone
who encompasses
love always.

STEP 2

Trust that love
can hold you.

STEP 3

Find a way to consciously
connect to your loving
light source every day.
Make it a habit.

STEP 4

When faced with a challenge, choose love first in your response.

STEP 5

Be love. Understand that those who fear love's potential don't need you to shield yourself, they need you to shine it on them so that they might free their own light.

STEP 6

Love deeper, love more, love yourself, love unconditionally.

Once you experience divine love and know that you have the power to access it when you choose to, that is a powerful realisation and there is no going back from that point. There is your life before that moment and your life afterwards and there is a significant divide between them.

EVERYTHING GROWS
THROUGH LOVE

The law of love. When we pour love into something, it grows, whether we do so consciously or subconsciously. When we tap into that loving energy, whatever is the recipient of that will grow. I want to give you a quirky little story about my hair, and it's just an example. You can apply this to more serious things, such as a connection with someone, getting a job, saving someone's life, healing someone.

I used to always get my hair done every week and it was always so healthy with a beautiful shine. I love my hair and I did this religiously. It was something I did for myself so obviously I was pouring love into my hair and it was benefiting and showing vibrancy. Happy hair!

When we moved to Australia, I was 35 weeks pregnant with my third child. Getting my hair done wasn't a priority on my list and of course I didn't have my regular hairdresser. Twelve years later, I started taking care of my hair again and every few months I'd go to the hairdresser's and get my hair blow dried but I couldn't justify the cost of having a colour or any other treatment.

Then it got to the stage where the business was going well so I decided to take every Thursday morning for me. The first thing on my agenda was to go and get my hair blow dried at 9 am every week. You know, I could blow dry it at home, but it never looks or feels the same. Taking that time out to sit and get something done for me is important to me, and it makes me feel good so I started booking in. Then I got a colour done at the hairdresser's and started getting six-weekly trims.

I had become used to thinking that my hair was not like it used to be and wishing that it would grow and that it was thicker. Yes, I know the power of thoughts, but sometimes you can't help yourself. And then suddenly I noticed that *Wow, my hair is getting thicker. Wow, my hair is getting longer. Wow, my hair looks and feels so healthy*. My kids were starting to notice it too, and they were saying, "Oh, Mommy's hair is so soft and so healthy."

I've been taking the time and giving some self-love to myself and to my hair that is actually important to me, so I've been reaping the rewards and I did it unconsciously.

If you just take a moment to stop and allow yourself to pour your love into something that matters to you, you see the benefits of it in many other ways. With my hair so much healthier I look better on camera so on Thursdays I schedule in making videos. That's become my video day. I'm more productive, more confident on video and I'm getting more contacts due to being more visible, which is attracting many more opportunities my way, all because I made the conscious decision to pour love into my hair.

I wasn't feeling good about my hair and this was blocking my mind from progressing. Think about what is blocked around you because you're not pouring love into some element of you. Ask yourself what matters to you, because what matters to you is important not only for you but for those around you. It's important for your business too, because when you pour love into yourself and what matters to you, everyone and everything benefits. It has a knock-on effect.

If something is calling and wants you to give more to it, stop and take the time to pour love into it, because the benefits will far outweigh any time commitment or financial sacrifice. Pour love into things and watch them grow.

LEAD WITH LOVE

I have been observing (and contributing) to a new type of leadership that is surging forward in our world. The inspired leader. These leaders are mission focused on making the world a better place, they see the bigger picture, they understand that there is no one size fits all approach to leadership, and being a leader is a privilege not an accolade. They show up even when the harsh leaders fear their strength and so try to knock them down. They lead with loving intention and know the power of connection, unity and bringing people together.

They are not afraid to share how they do things, it's not a secret to be them, it is a choice. This inspired leadership comes from leading by example, putting yourself in front, being courageous and most importantly being kind. An inspired leader never brings someone down to elevate themselves. An inspired leader rises higher by connecting wider with others, their agenda is aligned with their passion for having a positive impact on the world and it will be fused with their interests so that they can continue to fill their cup as they grow.

I believe this is a perfect blend of giving and receiving. We see many humanitarians giving so much of themselves that they end up sick or depleted, whereas a dictator or controlling leader thinks only of their own agenda and what they believe to be the right thing to do is always filling their own cup. An inspired leader considers all aspects of the decision, especially the balance between the desired outcome and the emotional toll and they know the importance of keeping themselves well so that they can serve at the highest capacity.

To lead with love inspired leaders embrace kindness and use it as a super power to move forward. Kindness is embedded deep in love and when we are kind we are also loving, so in turn we are leading through love.

New Zealand Prime Minister Jacinda Ardern is a great example of a leader who I believe leads with love. She doesn't shy away from the big decisions and has the courage to be kind. I loved watching how she led her country through a terrorist attack and also the global pandemic.

She ignores the call to be harsher in her navigation of her leadership. Even though what she has had to put in place may have felt harsh, she has delivered the solution with kindness and knowledge and has in turn inspired other nations to see the strength in this type of leadership so her nation responds well to her decisions because they feel part of the solution.

I am encouraged to see that there are so many more leaders in our world embracing loving values in their actions moving forward. This virtuous approach to leadership puts people at ease and helps to build trust within nations, within suburbs, within homes, within our hearts. It has a ripple effect from widespread to personal.

Let's all embrace a more loving approach to the way we lead.

THE GREATEST LOVE OF ALL - THE LOVE AFFAIR WITH OURSELVES.

The greatest love story of all is the love we have for ourselves. As a hopeless romantic I have learned the power of self-love, not in an egotistical 'I love myself' way but in the 'I am working with the divine energy of the universe' type of love. Love is the most productive energy of all. The vibration is so high that it can transcend dimensions and physical distance. If you tune into a loving frequency sent by a loved one, you can reap the benefits even if they are on the other side of the world.

I have to face the reality that being a mum of six and owning three publishing houses is busy but I like to take it in my stride as much as possible. A blend that I find works for me is to work throughout school terms and shift into a more relaxed mindset during school holidays when I have fun with my kids by day and I do some work in the early morning and evening if needed. I switch back into work mode after the school holidays.

Right now my kids have just finished their Term 3 holidays and so this present school term is all about getting ahead for me because their next holiday break will be six weeks over the summer. To make it productive for me I write during this time. We have a big backyard and I set up an outdoor desk for me and for them. It's so good for the soul. I have been doing this for five years and it works so I roll with it. My kids are getting older and when it comes to a time to transition this arrangement I will but for now I wouldn't change it for the world.

When I am in my work flow and I hit a day of overwhelm I close my diary and head to the beach for a walk. It is my happy place and I adore walking there, being near the ocean is so rejuvenating. I could stay at my desk and push through but that doesn't serve anyone well.

Are there times in your life when you could practise more self-care?

My tips for taking care of you:

1. Prioritise yourself as well as others.
2. If you are feeling overloaded take a break rather than pushing through.
3. It is your responsibility to take care of you.
4. Time for you does not need to be extravagant or pre-planned.
5. Know what your go-to instant recharge is and do more of that.
6. Get outside more and experience nature, it is an instant energy boost.

Why is it important to unconditionally love ourselves?

We cannot hope for others to love us when we don't love ourselves unconditionally. We have the ability to love ourselves unconditionally and through that love create a life that we love to live.

It is important to remember that we are the masters of our own happiness. I see many people hand over the keys to their happiness to someone else and that never works. Happiness is an inside job! Sure, others can make us happy, especially the life partners we choose, but it is our choice to be happy in that moment and to choose that person to share it with us. I am sure that many marriages break down because one partner has bestowed responsibility for their happiness onto the other partner and their expectations have not been met. Being responsible for someone else's happiness is hard work and can lead to resentment or failure and they are not high vibrational energies.

When we have a love affair with ourselves first, we show how we hope to be loved and how we can love another. That attracts the right person into our life, it emits from us like an energy vibration sending signals out that will ensure our heart's desire makes its way to us. Loving yourself first is one of the smartest things you will ever do.

HEAL THROUGH LOVE

"Love is the great miracle cure.
Loving ourselves works miracles in our lives."
Louise L. Hay.

I cannot speak about healing through love without mentioning the renowned Louise L. Hay. This lady encompassed loving energy, it emitted from every atom in her being. She opened my mind to healing at a whole new level, the healing ability we have within us.

When I experience an illness, discomfort or other physical woe I always ask myself what could be the underlying issue.

As self-help author and lecturer Bob Proctor shared in *The Secret*, disease cannot reside in a body that is in an emotionally balanced state. It may not be comforting to hear but it is interesting to discover that through love we can assist the healing process.

I say assist because I am a great believer that conventional medicine was created by scientists through their love for humanity, so it is an important approach to treating illness but it is not the only way.

It is important that we choose to pour love, not fear, into ourselves or our loved ones who are unwell. Many people go instantly into fear and that is understandable as a diagnosis of serious illness can instigate a shock reaction. However, when we live through love, we can guide ourselves or our loved ones into a more emotionally healing state, one filled with hope. Try to focus on a healthy outcome together and let the doctors deal with the illness, because when an illness consumes your mind as well as your body, healing potential is delayed.

The work of researcher, lecturer and author Dr Joe Dispenza may help navigate you inwards toward the miraculous healing potential that each of us has. His story is phenomenal. He speaks about how you can regenerate and heal at a cellular level.

To find out morfe, visit his website
https://drjoedispenza.com/

LOVE AND SUCCESS

There is no more powerful energy that you can put into the pursuit of your success than love. When we do things with loving intention, people can feel it. They end up supporting us more on our quest and they can see the passion, the flame within us burning with the desire of what we want to achieve.

Napoleon Hill's book *Think and Grow Rich* took twenty-five years to research and write. This book is a labour of love. Can you imagine that much of your life being dedicated to collecting and analysing stories from people across the world? This book has now become the foundation of so many success strategies worldwide. If you're going to do anything for yourself and your success journey, whether it's in pursuit of the perfect career, in entrepreneurship or anything else, you need to read, this book.

Bob Proctor who owned Procter Gamble Institute studied Think and Grow Rich for fifty years. He studied it every day, dropping in and out of it. It's a book that I want engraved within my knowledge bank because every time I read or listen to it, something else resonates. Hill's premise is that *your thoughts, whether positive or negative, become your reality. You must control your thoughts if you want to control your destiny.* A foundation has developed around the book and there are now many people associated with delivering its teachings and their perspectives on the principles it presents. It is one of the books on the reading list that you'll find at the back of this book.

We all learn from each other. Napoleon Hill put this book together not to make a million dollars, but to respond to the call and answer the question of what successful people had in common.

And he took on that quest. He took on the challenge and it took him twenty-five years to fulfil it. Now, I imagine it was wonderful interviewing these amazing humans who have achieved so much and Hill's perspective is insightful but he could never have foreseen the book's success or that it would touch millions of lives and continue to have an impact for decades to come. *Think and Grow Rich* is now a movie and there is also a magazine in which I recently shared my own story.

I encourage you to read this book. It will give you a foundation for success that you could never have imagined. And think of the power of what you can achieve if you really put love into what you are pursuing. We plant seeds of intention and then we nurture the opportunities and follow up on the inspired thoughts that come when those seeds are planted. We nurture them to flourish with love.

It reminds me of an experiment conducted with two batches of seeds. One batch was nurtured, given water, light, whatever they needed scientifically to grow. The other batch also had their basic requirements met but with the addition of being talked to and having a lot of loving energy directed to them. The seeds that were nurtured with loving energy grew bigger, brighter, healthier than the seeds that were supplied with only their basic needs.

Think about that for a moment. Think of the power of that energy. Why would you choose to put any other energy into what you are growing? Think about your children. If you don't have children, think about when you were a child. I know whenever I think about my children, I feel so much love for them. They know they're loved unconditionally. Why? I know the value of unconditional love because I was gifted it as a child and it was only as I grew up that I realised not everyone experienced this.

That foundation of knowing that you're unconditionally loved is the greatest gift of all, no matter a family's wealth. As children, we had everything we needed but not a lot of extras. I did have that unconditional love and that is a gift. The greatest gift of all is love and it helped me to grow into the person I am today.

And I want to give and I want to share my love with everyone because love is infinite. We cannot run out of it. The more that we give, the more we have to give. Living with an open heart requires courage. You need to know yourself better than anyone else knows you so that you can stand true to yourself and not get caught up with negativity.

Sometimes in being true to yourself and being loving those people who are not ready to receive that will not react as you hope. But that's not about you. That's them. When you're on the success tangent, surround yourself with your people, the people who love to receive what you give and love to raise you up. That is love. That is success.

We're always on a quest for success because we're ever evolving, and when we achieve one thing we roll onto a new cycle and we're at the beginning of something new again. So we're forever progressing and love is sharing that. We are here to share what we learn with others. I have people who say to me, "Are you are you crazy? Why do you show people how to publish their own books?"

Why would I keep that to myself? If somebody is willing to put in the work that I put in, then they deserve the results that I get. If everyone finds their way there's no competition. When we show up and share and help someone on their journey to make it easier for them, that is something wonderful and that has to be celebrated. That is love, sharing and caring. It's not only the one person who receives it. Everyone around them benefits and the ripples of one absolute definite act of love are widespread. That is why we need to be open to receiving. It took me a while to learn that I was always the giver.

I like to give. It makes me feel good so I receive in that way. But

I also understand that I have to be able to receive from others who choose to gift me. There's nothing wrong with that. It's beautiful.

Only you know your personal definition of success, whether it is in business, love, lifestyle. For me, success is having this beautiful balance between family and ambition. I'm an ambitious person. I like to achieve things. It makes me feel good. I like to help people and financial stability is part of that because if I'm earning well, then I'm able to do more. That's what money is for, to keep things going, not for hoarding away.

It's for keeping the wheels in motion, because as we need it, the money will come to make those things happen. There is success in loving my children, loving myself, loving where I am in life, loving what I do, just loving my life. Yet my life could be someone else's nightmare.

I'm not joking. I'm a mom of six. I live in a little house not far from the beach. It's beautiful here in Perth, Australia. I feel so grateful. But you can look at the other side of it. There's never a moment where it's not busy. There's always something to do. But I was gifted a beautiful gift from my mother and I'm able to switch off in between things so that my mind can be calm when needed.

I live on the other side of the world from my family and I miss them. I don't focus on that because now is not the time for me to put energy into them because I can't take action on that. What I can take action on is my beautiful life that I have created by design for myself and my family. And each member of my family may choose to design their life differently, but they will feel supported on that. For me being a successful parent is guiding my children, not controlling them. And each of them is different. Yes, it takes more effort on my part, but to watch them grow up into beautiful individuals, for me that is success.

Everyone has different priorities in their success quest so understand what that is for you. When you understand what success means to you, that is in itself success. Enjoy.

LOVE AND RELATIONSHIPS

I have always been a difficult person to be in a relationship with and not because I'm unlovable. In fact, the love that I give is so pure, so, so pure that it really connects with those I gift it to and it's absolutely genuine. The reason I'm hard to be with is that I don't need somebody else's love to be validated. I already love myself and I know that is enough.

When I choose to receive love, it's powerful. When our love comes together, it is a powerful energy that when projected into something united is mind blowing and effective. I don't say this lightly. It's from experience. I'm a total romantic and the dynamics of love when two people come together, the energy exchange, the connection, you don't question that when it's true love.

You may pinch yourself and wonder, "Oh, my goodness, is this happening" but when you embrace it, don't overthink it and simply bask in the essence of it, that is the most beautiful thing ever. Of course, as humans we overcomplicate things and destroy things and self-sabotage. And that's tragic. But when we show up in love and connect in love and that's reciprocated, that is special and should never be questioned, judged, or sabotaged in any way.

When two loving energies combine, they create life and that's a miracle. When my first child was delivered into the world, I felt like my heart could burst with love. As a mum of six, I thought, "Oh my goodness, am I going to have enough love to give?"

Absolutely. You know, I have enough love to give the whole globe if they're receptive of it. There's nothing like a hug. I love hugging my children. I get so much out of it when our hearts connect. It's a physical feeling and one that the kids need. My fifteen-year-old still comes to me for a hug. And it's not just a quick hug, it's an actual hug filled with love that pours into them because they need it, because being a teenager is tough when you are getting to know who you are.

Love needs to be reciprocated, to be given equally on both sides for it to be this beautiful harmony that creates more **beautiful things in our world.** But it's OK for you to stand in love for yourself and know yourself and know that you are love, that you have that to give their confidence.

Some people may feel inadequate, they may feel things about that, and that's so sad.

When we all truly take time to stand in our own love within ourselves and love ourselves first, everyone benefits because then we set a precedent on how we deserve to be loved. Sparks fly when two people get together and they make love. Is that not the most beautiful, sensual thing that you can ever give to someone?

It's like an aphrodisiac. It's like a drug, an absolute euphoria. Exploration of each other's bodies comes into play because you can trust each other, and the most beautiful connection happens because of that love.

When it stands the test of time there's nothing more beautiful than a couple in their eighties or nineties looking at each other adoringly because they know they're loved, they love each other. You can be guaranteed they have had a lifetime of ups and downs and maybe were on the brink of divorce at times, but they've come through it and they are there together at the end of their lifetime, still loving each other, accepting and honouring that love.

Love needs to start with yourself, really knowing and loving yourself and allowing that love to flow through you first and then pour into others.

Take a moment to stop and look at your relationship with yourself. Do you love yourself? Flaws and all? My goodness, I am not perfect. No way. But I know what I want and how to get it. I know how to give and how to have that balance between giving and receiving. I know how to love and I know how to pour back into myself when I need to.

I know the value of keeping my cup full so that I can pour love into others. Don't sacrifice too much of yourself so that you are left depleted because that is of no use to anybody. As I write this, I am sitting in bed snuggled up because I have a head cold. I don't want it to last long so I've taken to my bed to work. Already I feel better because I'm talking about love and love is all healing.

So think about your relationship with yourself and others and how you want those relationships to be and pour love into that. See what happens, what flourishes.

LOVING ENERGY AS YOUR SUPER FUEL

Numerous times a day, I use loving energy as a super fuel. Of course, I need to ensure that I have a never-ending supply to use and that is where the self-love chapter comes in handy. When you harness this energy to achieve your desires or help someone, something beautiful happens.

When I set an intention, I will also inject some loving energy in there to get it started and when inspired thoughts and opportunities aligned with that intention present themselves to me I have the courage to say yes to the YES's and NO to the definite no's and the distracting maybe's.

Choosing love is a choice, you can equally choose hate, but I hope that after reading this book you won't. From my experience of making amazing things happen in my life I will always choose love. Not only do I get more satisfying results I also get to live through a higher vibration which is turn gifts me happiness

Most of us strive for happiness but seek it externally when in fact happiness comes from within. No external source should be in control of your happiness. The gatekeeper of your happiness must be you because your internal navigation system works one hundred per cent in your favour, not only to benefit you but also everyone around you. When someone bestows the control of their happiness on us, or we do the same to someone else it is an unfair expectation because they don't beat through your heart.

Connecting to love in order to achieve your heart's desire, whatever that may be, is something you can all do instantly when you learn how.

When you choose to react through love every time it has an impact beyond any thought capacity we have, it ripples further and wider than we could ever know. But we actually don't need to know in order to receive the benefits in our life. All you need to know is that when you choose to react with love only good things come from that.

My tips for harnessing love as a super fuel are:

1. Learn how to react with love; make love a habit.
2. Be open to all goodness that comes your way.
3. Accept energetic and physical gifts with huge gratitude.
4. Accept compliments with gratitude.
5. When unsure of what to do, think "what would love do?"
6. Understand that you don't need to understand. Love is not a thinking process, it is an open-hearted process.

One of the key things to note about loving energy is that there is an unlimited supply. Love multiplies the more we use it. It is miraculous like that. I never try to understand that, I just allow myself to know it.

When you live choosing love, if you stumble in life you never fall so far that you can't dust yourself off and get back on track.

A LOVE FUELLED EXPERIENCE

I want to share with you a love fuelled experience I had recently. I'm usually the person who creates the events, hosts people there and creates the experience. This time the call was loud for me to go and bask in the energy and experience of an Ausmumpreneur retreat with the amazing Katy Gardner and Peace Mitchell. I was going to relax, recharge and rejuvenate my energy because I was at capacity.

I know myself well enough to know when I need to stop. A big thing for me is leaving my family, and I don't like to be away from them too long but I knew that to be my best self, I needed to go away and recalibrate. I just knew I had to go so I set the intention. My husband knows whenever something calls me like this there's no point trying to talk me out of it. He went along with it even though flying to the other side of Australia in the middle of a pandemic wasn't ideal. Any number of scenarios could happen including finding myself in a fourteen-day lockdown and unable to return home, all for the sake of three nights to recharge and recalibrate.

I could have gone to a local hotel in Perth and written my heart out for three days or simply recharged. But that wasn't the way it was supposed to happen. I needed to go and experience this retreat for the divinity that was to come with it. A lot of serendipitous things came into play, a lot of unexpected alignments. I was adamant that I wanted to get a direct flight from Western Australia to Queensland, even though that meant I would arrive thirty-six hours before the retreat.

Now, a significant number for me is 22. I think of it as 'my' number. My house is number 22 in our street. Exciting things often happen for me connected with 22 and I know big things are going to happen this year especially as we move into 2022 with the alignment of numbers. What I didn't realise until I arrived there was that the retreat was being held on the twenty-second week of the year. I just knew I had to be there.

Luckily I listened to my knowing because I went over and Katy picked me up and I spent a day with these two amazing women followed by a night on my own, the first time I had been alone in a house in more than twenty years.

Wow. There I was in a beautiful little beachside bungalow beside Mission Beach, Queensland, which is the energy porthole of Australia. I hadn't known that. Then during the retreat there was a full moon lunar eclipse. Twenty women came together and this divine thing was happening in the energy porthole of Australia. Holy moly.

It was such a life changing experience. From the moment I was picked up to the moment I left, every single thing Katy and Peace did was with loving intention. Everything was fuelled through love, down to the minutest details such as how things would be positioned to exclusive cutlery in each bungalow.

Every single detail was put together with so much loving intention. Every experience we had was felt through that love and not one thing went wrong. It was flawless. Obviously, behind the scenes of events things do go wrong, but everything flowed and was as it should have been.

Every experience was harnessed and embraced. I only went there to rejuvenate, hang out with amazing women and just recharge yet I had breakthroughs myself even though I felt that I was pretty much together. Of course, we're always a powerful work in motion, regardless of the goals we achieve. We're always evolving. We're always going through these cycles of evolution and that retreat marked the start of a new cycle for me, the merging of my business and my authorship.

I'm successful and I'm comfortable and confident in my authorship because I know that what I am sharing changes lives. It connects with and inspires people. But imagine that you've been working ten years in your employment. You're really confident, you've really built traction and brand awareness and lots of people want to work with you.

You have this presence. You show up authentically and confidently in that space alongside people. And then you're called to something else because you've got all of the publishing wrapped up, you've worked to bring it to a certain place and it's there. You're able to serve well, but you've now made room for magic. That's what was happening. The call to share, to start putting energy into my writing and to show authors what can happen when you do put yourself all in to your project.

I showed up at this retreat perceived by everyone as the publisher but I was really there as the author and the two merged because of the loving environment that was created for that merger to flourish. I experienced breakthroughs because I had the space and clarity to embrace them and also harvested the insight and knowledge that came through the other participants.

That was their gift to me because of the amazing energy and connection we had. It was super powerful. The two worlds of my authorship and my business collided and were embraced. Before I left spoke at a business conference attended by Queensland government representatives and heard later that one of the attendees considered my talk the highlight of the presentations.

The universe sends affirmations when you on the right path, signs to let you know to keep going. That was my signpost. But the ultimate thing was the love that fuelled that retreat. And I know how much energy it takes to put in that kind of loving intention that comes from the most authentic place.

Genuine, absolutely. Giving heart bliss. Yeah. So be mindful of the experiences you create. If you're creating events, harness and embrace all the love you can and inject that into the event. I promise you your event will stay with people much longer. Attending this retreat was such a deep, profound experience for me. I always inject love into my events and will now be injecting so much more because of the inspiration I gained and what I experienced.

So it has a ripple effect. Imagine if you have twenty or a hundred or a thousand people experiencing that love-fuelled event and each one of them taking something away from it and creating that experience for somebody else. That's the foundation for change. That's the foundation for love to ripple through our world.

That's when we feel at home and that we belong. That's when we feel loved and cherished. And that is what we all should be able to feel openly without any overthinking, without ever feeling awkward. That's the kind of genuine connection we should be promoting around this amazing world.

Can you identify a love-fuelled experience you have had recently?

THE ANSWER IS LOVE

The answer is 'LOVE'.

What is the question?

What is the key to true happiness?

We all strive to be happy. No matter what circles we revolve in, our main goal is happiness. Whether it is materialistic or ambitious our end goal is achieving something that makes us, as individuals, feel happy. Many people strive for perfection. But who is it that determines what perfection is? We all have our own ideals of perfection and aim for that, and why? To make us HAPPY!

Now armed with this information that feeling love makes us happy, what are you going to do about it? How do you get enough love to make you happy? I am pleased to tell you that you don't need to go seeking it; you just need to unlock the vault to your own self-love. By loving ourselves we will discover true happiness that no amount of material possessions will ever give us. When we access this love we will discover there is a never-ending supply all for ourselves that we can share with others and it will never dry up. In fact the more we spread our love, the more that is created and the more that comes back to us.

I like to think of it as a snowball. By starting off with a little ball of love and giving it the opportunity to grow by rolling it along and nurturing it, we enable it to become a greater ball of love. Then in no time at all it will be ready to roll down the mountain of life gathering more and more love all of the time. What do we have at the end? A great BIG ball of Love that everyone can feel and enjoy. Did you know we can heal our body and mind just by loving ourselves? Simply by taking the time to listen to the signals your body is giving, you have the power within you to perform miraculous things.

"Love creates miracles, Love creates magic."
Sascha Brooks

According to author Louise L. Hay, by loving yourself and affirming this love through positive affirmations you can heal ANY ailment or illness you may have. Yes, it is that amazing!

Tips on how to love yourself

Self-love may sound easy to do, but it is a process that needs focus and time to blossom. People who have suffered childhood neglect and abuse will find it difficult to take the steps towards self-love. Here are some tips I came across to assist in overcoming these steps.

- Compile a list of things OTHERS like about you. Ask people who know and love you what they like about you. This is a first step towards realising your personal qualities. Write your own list of what YOU like about yourself. Be honest with yourself. If you are having trouble, think about the people you love and the qualities you admire in them. Do you have those same qualities?
- Create a feel-good notebook/box. Invest in a notebook or box that makes you feel good when you see it. Use it to keep these lists. Look at its contents every time you feel low or if you are made to feel low by someone else.
- Read these lists often. Make reading these wonderful things about you a regular occurrence in your life as often as you can. Every time you do, it will eliminate one time you felt bad or were made to feel bad and replace it with a positive.

- Add a note. Make yourself tune in to hearing the positives about yourself, no longer the negatives. Write each of them down and add them to your collection.
- You are your own best friend. We all love our friends but I have news for you: YOU are your own best friend. Love yourself as you do your friends. Close your eyes, feel the love you have for them and project it onto yourself. Store that feeling.
- Give yourself a break. Learn to be compassionate and forgiving to yourself. Would you be so hard and judgmental on your friends or loved ones? No, you would probably be there offering support. Feel that love and compassion for yourself.
- Love comes from within. A well of love exists within us all and we can access it whenever we choose. Access self-love regularly. You deserve to be loved, so love yourself.
- Affirmations. By using affirmations you are registering positives in your brain which will help you to feel good. Things like: I am an amazing, loving and caring person. I deserve the very best in my life. Pin them up in the areas you are in most often—your car, computer, fridge, at work. Feel them.
- Nurture yourself. Do things for yourself that make you feel loved and cared for. A nice pampering session, some meditation, a wonderful book, a peaceful walk. These are some things we can gift to ourselves that will enhance our loving potential.
- Listen. Take a quiet moment to listen to yourself and the signs you are receiving. It may take time to connect but by giving yourself some time each day to listen to your inner guide you will more easily recognise your needs and desires.

- Look. This will be a hard one for many. I know it was for me. Look in a mirror; look straight into your eyes and tell yourself "I love you". Do this every day as often as you feel comfortable and you will find it will get easier. I found it very emotional the first time I did it. For me the eyes are the gateway to the soul and I felt an intense feeling at that moment.

These are all tips you can use to assist on your journey to self-love. You need only select those you feel will work for you. It can be hard to give yourself this gift at first but always know that you have the courage and strength within you and you deserve it! The love you attract from others comes from you initially. If you don't love yourself then it is really hard for others to love you.

I know this because I went through a period where I did not take the time to love me. I was just motoring along, loving my family and doing what I thought was right. But it wasn't OK. My relationships were straining around me and I was not being fulfilled, my soul was perishing. Since learning to love myself, I radiate love and in every aspect of my life all of my relationships have blossomed too. I have so much love now within and I know that I will always glow.

When I talk about loving myself I don't mean being arrogant; this is when someone thinks only of themself. No, self-love is when someone has a strong sense of respect for and confidence in themselves. This is usually taught in childhood through honesty, acceptance and unconditional love. However most parents have their own issues of self-doubt and limiting beliefs which they project onto their children consciously and unconsciously and so a cycle of self-rejection repeats itself.

So let's break the cycle and the stigma attached to self-love. In order to truly love another we need to first love ourselves. It is important not only for us but for our families and for humanity.

Everything in life will be better now that we know 'The Answer'.

"Love is the great miracle cure. Loving ourselves works miracles in our lives."
Louise L Hay

The Gift
of Gratitude

*There is always something to be
grateful for, even on the darkest day
there will be light.*

THE GRATITUDE FORMULA

There is a formula to gratitude that is quite simple in its theory yet often complicated for many in its application. I have found that it is a mindset that allows for a rhythm that gives way to a habit of productive gratitude.

Gratitude + emotion + focused intentions + aligned action = a winning gratitude formula.

You can't lose when you tap into this high frequency energetic vibration.

Gratitude alone will get results but if you want to experience next level experiences you will first be in the energy of gratitude and allow the essence of the emotions you are feeling to ripple through you so that you are emitting a high energy frequency. It is at this point when you should navigate some energy into what you want to manifest in your future. Then when inspired thoughts and/or opportunities aligned with those intentions present themselves to you, you will know. If you have the courage to action them straight away you will achieve results higher than you can ever imagine.

GRATITUDE

Take a moment to think in your mind and feel in your heart what you are grateful for in your life. Even someone experiencing the direst existence has the opportunity to tap into gratitude with the fact that they are alive. If that is all you can muster it is still something to be grateful for and can be used as a catalyst to manifest great things in your life if you allow it to do so.

Being grateful is a wonderful virtue and also an amazing tool for positioning yourself where you want to be in the future. You need to be grateful now for whatever you wish to experience in your life in order to have it in your future. It is a beautiful cycle that when you allow it to flow will create bucket loads of magic in your life.

EMOTION

One of the best ways to regulate high vibrational emotions is to prioritise joy as much as possible.

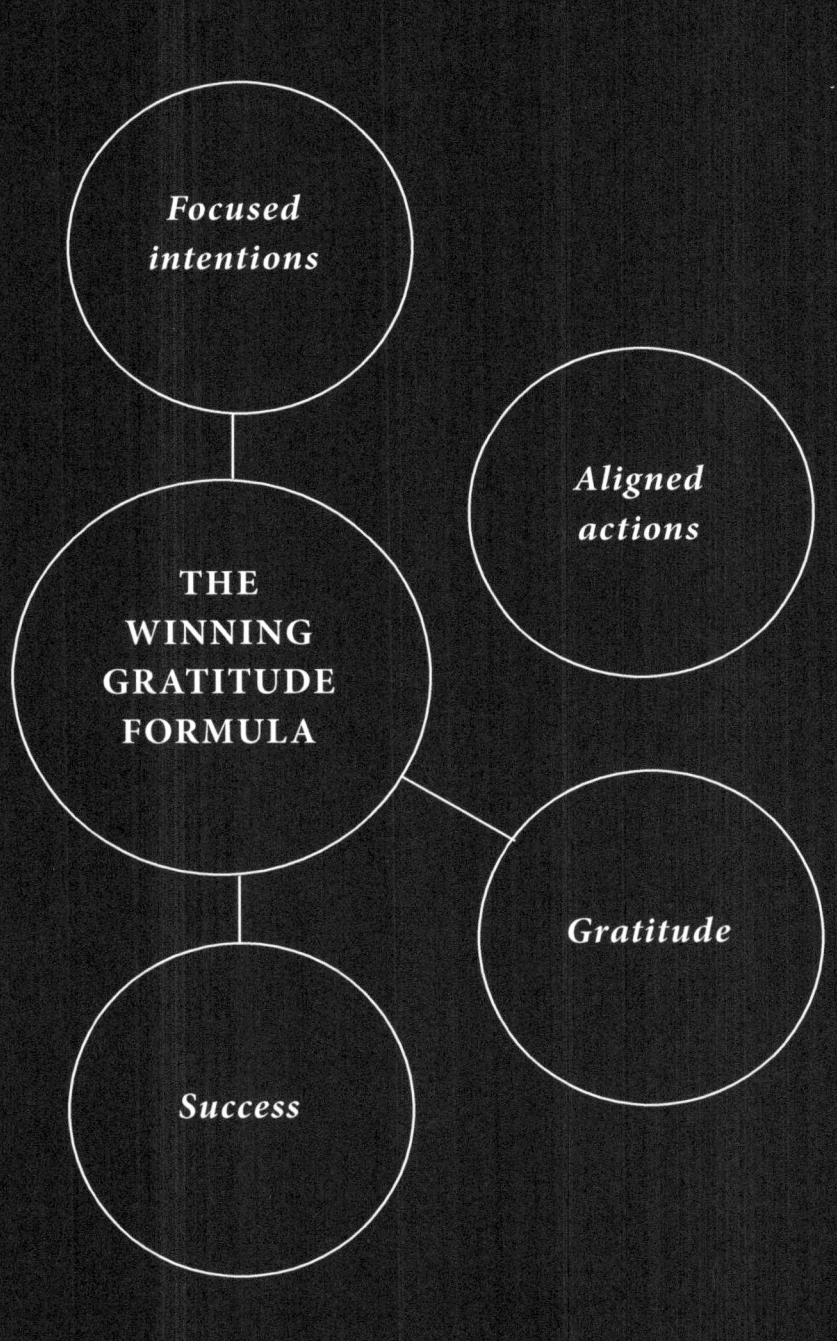

WHY GRATITUDE?

Gratitude is an instant hack into the flow of abundance. When you are grateful for something with all of your heart you can attract more of that goodness into your life. Most people do not understand the power of gratitude but the big thing here is that you don't need to understand it, you simply need to embrace it.

Over thinking things is a block to receiving. We need to allow things to be and trust that they are exactly as they need to be but of course, as humans we tend to overcomplicate things. It's in our genetics.

When I am asked, *why gratitude?* I reply, *why not?* Embrace gratitude and see the benefits you experience in your life.

I used to be one of those people who didn't value gratitude enough so I decided to be a test dummy and see what would happen if I became more grateful. Coming from a Catholic background I already knew how to say night-time prayers that were filled with gratitude, so I gave that a modern spin and sat in gratitude before I went to sleep every night. What was profound is that I instantly saw a difference in my life. Things became more positive from the get go. My relationship with my kids was much better and when I was grateful for the material things I had, I ended up with more. I knew it was to do with my new daily practice but I couldn't understand the logistics of it. The results were there so I decided to embrace it and so I say to you, don't overcomplicate things. Embrace this and the results will speak for themselves.

Ask yourself *why gratitude?* for you. What do you believe gratitude could bring into your daily life? Then prioritise it and watch the magic happen. Gratitude brings instant results into the lives of those who choose to see. As with everything in life, we need to choose gratitude every day. I have reaped the rewards for being steadfast with gratitude. Some days were easier than others but being mindful to be grateful every day was one of the best choices I have ever made. It had the power to turn what seemed to be a negative experience of life into a positive experience by helping me back on track after a dark period when I fell below the line and gratitude was not easy. But just because it wasn't easy didn't mean it was impossible, and each step towards gratitude took me a step further from the darkness. So whether you are investing in your mental wealth security deposit bank or trying to find your way out of the darkness, gratitude is a worthwhile investment every time! That is why you should choose gratitude!

An attitude of gratitude

Every action has an equal reaction so when you approach others and situations with an attitude of gratitude you can't lose.

Gratitude is a high vibrational choice. It's easy when reacting to an act of kindness but not so easy when it comes to actioning it without a catalyst, so choosing gratitude takes effort in the beginning. Some people have been brought up to be grateful through modems such as prayer and this is good practice but not the productive type of gratitude.

It keeps us humble and mindful of others and the small things in life. My issue with this is that it keeps us small, and the potential energy emitted from the gratitude we express is not channelled into our dreams so that we can make great things happen in our lives.

We need to have an attitude of gratitude that serves us because in doing so it will ripple out to our families, communities, and the world. The ripple effect of gratitude is always rooted in goodness, and we need more of that!

When it comes to being grateful it's so much easier when it is part of our DNA, but if it isn't part of your nature don't lose faith, for with a bit mindfulness it will be. We cannot be in control of our past experience but we can be an influence on what we aspire to be and experience in our future and that starts today. Gratitude is a constant opportunity for us to show up in life. The potential energy awaiting us in every moment of gratitude, whether it be in embracing gratitude from another person or expressing gratitude ourselves, is an epic gift.

1. For the highest potential to flow, it is important to both be able to gift gratitude;
2. and most importantly, to receive it.

The significance of this is paramount to maintaining a high vibration in our lives. It's a circular exchange that we need not think about too much but it is beneficial to be aware of the power of this simplistic interaction so that we don't become blocks. Allow gratitude to flow in your life to and from others and the results will be visible in no time. Embrace an attitude of gratitude every day!

HOW GRATITUDE
CAN SERVE YOU

Gratitude is a choice, a smart choice. You could spend all of your time having battles with people, living at a low vibration and fighting your way through life, or you can choose to come from a higher stance and inject gratitude into everything you do. Gratitude is more than a choice. It's a feeling, it's an essence. It becomes part of you.

Make the choice to embrace gratitude. If it's a struggle for you initially, create it as a habit. Do a 21-day habit challenge where you practise gratitude mindfully for 21 days, and it then becomes a subconscious habit. It becomes easier and second nature for you. But how gratitude can serve you is when you allow it to become part of you, and then you make choices through that. And the reason that it serves you is because:

1. It comes from a really good energetic manifestation space.
2. You'll always get the best-case scenario out of anything that you apply it to, whether that is an interaction, an intention or a goal, and whether it is for yourself or others.

When you embrace gratitude, you are at peace with the world, you are in a state of flow. You end up in a very high vibration because not only is gratitude one of the highest virtues, it's also productive and will serve you well. So if you're smart, you will embrace gratitude in your life because it will serve you, it will get you results.

When you are grateful with an open heart and there is love behind it, people will feel that energy and that action will cause a positive reaction in most cases. Sometimes it will conjure up things within others that they don't like about themselves and that can lead to a negative reaction, but they're not your people so don't give them any energy. Save your gratitude for those people who react beautifully to it.

And that's how gratitude serves you. It serves you well, as in, you show up, you put the energy into it because it does require energy. If you put the energy into it, you will get the results in all aspects of your life. Here is an example that comes to mind, and you can check this out in the gratitude stories at the end of this book.

I had a conversation about gratitude with Intuitive Life and Business Coach Joanna Hunter. Joanna talks about how people like to feel appreciated, and when you have appreciation for each other, then the to-ing and fro-ing between you, the interactions between you come from a more genuine place, a place of love. Whereas whenever someone doesn't feel appreciated, they can become resentful. I know that when I apply gratitude to any interaction with anybody I connect with, I always get a better response no matter what.

I always choose gratitude but not overly in-your-face, swamping-you gratitude, just honest down to Earth goodness. It's become second nature. Now gratitude beams from me because I embrace it. And I love it when someone feels gratitude for me, I love the reaction. Even if I don't get the usual reaction, I love to give gratitude because when it lands with someone, it shifts something within them.

Maybe they're not used to receiving that type of energy sent their way but you've made a change. You've ignited something and even if it's an initial rejection, it's still there. They'll carry it forward with them. And that's pretty special.

Gratitude is a gift to the world and a gift to yourself as it will always serve you. People will remember you as the person who gifted that to them because people always remember how you made them feel rather than the details of your interaction. Gratitude serves us well in both business and personal forums.

It serves me well as a mother. Maybe I'm frustrated because I've got some work on and I need a bit of space to do it but my kids are looking for my energy. There's no point doing battle with that. I may as well stop, close the computer and give them some energy, let them know how grateful I am for them and pour my love into them.

It's a mindfulness, a choice. I could sit and try to get the work done, but I would never get anything worthwhile done in that energy and I'm always mindful of that. When I choose to close the computer and be grateful and show gratitude to my children, that's when I get the best out of them. They are pure, pure form, and they are there to test the boundaries. They are there for us to see the best and the worst in ourselves. That's what children do because they are growing. They're curious. They are true energy and sometimes without a filter. Most of us have been conditioned so much by the time we reach adulthood that we do need to reconnect with our inner child. We also need to embrace the essence of gratitude with our children. By me showing it to my children, they can show it back to me.

Make the right decision. Choose gratitude and let it serve you.

GRATITUDE AND MONEY

When you're grateful for the money you have, you will automatically without conscious effort be creating an energetic flow that comes back to you because with every action there's always a reaction. It's all part of the universal laws. Whether or not you know it and are working consciously with those laws, if you have a positive grateful thought about the money you already have in your life, then you will experience more money coming back in.

That's how it goes. There's no point overthinking it. The money that comes into your life as a result of that positive energy is beautiful money. More good people in the world need to think good things about money, because when good people have money, good things happen.

It's important to remember that. When you're grateful for what you have and open to receiving, can you imagine what can happen? Imagine what conscious gratitude around money would help to bring about in your life. We've talked about gratitude and the law of attraction. If you are thinking about the money you want to have in the future, you don't think about the lack of it in the present.

You need to be fully in the gratitude and the energy of what it would be like to have more money in your life. Sit in that energy, in a present mindful moment, really consciously owning and thinking about what your life would be like. What would the essence of your life be like if you had the money you wanted? It needs to be believable for you.

One of my Seven Life Principles is belief. You need to believe it is possible for you to have all the money you want in your life. If you're just dreaming while believing it's impossible, then it will never be possible. If you think it's beyond you, it will always be beyond you. It's important to sit in the energy of what you want so that it's completely believable for you to experience it, because the only limitations on what you can achieve are those you put on yourself. Quite often that is due to limiting beliefs or past experiences.

So do it slowly. Raise your gratitude for money and be grateful for the money you have now, but consciously be grateful for the money you want to have in your future by feeling what it would be like to already have it. My heart flutters with absolute excitement when I think of what I have, what I'm going to have in my future. Just remember, money doesn't bring happiness, but money does bring opportunities for happiness to happen.

It's not bad to have nice things. It's actually beautiful to be opulent, and it's so much more fulfilling and rewarding. When the money comes from a good source, you've earned it or you've manifested it in a beautiful way. So why not you? If it's not you, it'll be somebody else. Money is a positive in your life if you allow it to be by being grateful for it.

We all know how to be grateful. But do you know how to be consciously grateful? This book will show you how.

Embrace it. Enjoy it. It's there for all to have should we choose it.

GRATITUDE AND KINDNESS

Kindness is important to discuss around the subject of gratitude because they are both of the same essence. When kindness walks hand in hand with gratitude, beautiful things happen. A little quote that came into my arena recently about kindness is that kindness is someone who brings warmth and value to somebody with no expectation in return. That's why gratitude walks so beautifully with kindness, because the to-ing and fro-ing of giving and receiving without any expectation is something beautiful.

I love giving. I receive a lot in giving energetically, but a lot of people don't understand or see that depth in giving. Some people give to receive. That's not me. I don't give with any expectation, because whenever somebody does choose to react it doesn't always happen in that moment. Sometimes it's not an instant reaction.

Some people like to simply tick the box of giving. But if you think about the kindness of giving from an energetic, universal laws perspective, Karma refers to what you give out coming back to you. It does though it either comes back to you from the person you give it to or goes to another. We shouldn't try to control that with expectation because time and circumstance align and that's where the magic happens.

Just because we choose to give something to someone, it may not be the right time for them to give to us. They may not be in a good place. They may need kindness shone down upon them, and they will carry it in their hearts, and they will find a way to repay you. And that is beautiful. If you are a person who expresses kindness, don't stop because someone doesn't understand the universal laws and the flow around it. Don't stop the flow. We need that energetic flow in our world.

If you are someone who blocks kindness, if kindness makes you feel uncomfortable, maybe think about it a different way. You could choose gratitude rather than repelling the kindness because gratitude allows it to free flow onto a very high energetic vibration which will serve you and also the person who's being kind. Why would you not choose that more than another negative way?

One time I was in a shop and didn't grab my groceries and go. I had a high vibe happening that day, and as I walked down one of the aisles there was a woman stacking shelves. I said, 'Hello, how are you going today?' It caught her off guard and she smiled back and said, 'I am fine. Thank you for asking.' It lifted her spirits.

I expected nothing in return and it wouldn't have mattered if she didn't smile back. I was just going to infuse that kindness into her day because I got a sense that she needed it. We don't need validation to be kind. We just need to be kind.

I have the pleasure of working alongside the amazing, beautiful Duchess of York. She's the Kindness Ambassador, and is one of the kindest people I know. She's very mindful of others.

We need to open ourselves up and allow our children to understand the value in kindness and all the virtues. We need to bring it into the schools. We need to understand the value of kindness at a younger age so it becomes second nature to us. Let's do that. Let's embrace kindness. It's not giving yourself to somebody, it's pouring that energy into another. And my goodness, it pours back into you.

Did you know we can talk about the kindness quotient in the same way as there is an intelligence quotient or IQ? Have you ever thought about what your kindness quotient might be? I invite you to use the link below to find out your KQ. How kind are you? Be honest with the questions. And I'd love for you to come to the Life Magic with KP Weaver FB group and share your Kindness Quotient.

THE SCIENCE OF GRATITUDE

There is a great deal of research around the science of gratitude and how beneficial it is for us, and I'll share links at the back of this book. I want to keep it basic here so feel free to do your own research. I'm sharing research that resonates with my heart because what resonates with my heart often resonates with my readers' hearts.

I don't like to get things too complicated so let's focus on the wonderful things that gratitude brings into our lives and the science behind it. Did you know that gratitude increases happiness by 25%? Many of us strive for happiness every day so if you want to be happier, start bringing gratitude into your life.

Did you know that gratitude improves your health? Studies show that a grateful mind is linked to healthier blood pressure and heart rate, as well as a stronger immune system and less aches and pains. It's because feeling gratitude and having a happier heart reduces our stress levels and that has a wonderful impact on our health.

People who express gratitude sleep better. This positive trait leads to better quality and longer sleep. When you look at the research, there are very good reasons to practise gratitude from a health point of view — decreased blood pressure, especially for those with hypertension, increased energy levels, reduced stress and physical symptoms, improved sleep quality and a longer life expectancy.

In business, you achieve goals faster, you're more productive, you have fewer sick days, you're better focused, you retain customers, and are more prosperous. From a self-learning perspective, you're more optimistic about yourself. Feeling gratitude benefits your brain and improves your memory, making learning easier. It has a positive effect on relationships, leading to deeper, more thoughtful connections and kinder interactions with others. When you're grateful, all of those things come into play.

Research shows gratitude has a positive effect on all those areas of your life — your health, your business and career, your finances, self-learning and your relationships. They all come together and flow and blend together. You can focus on one aspect but gratitude covers them all. It enhances them all. Why would you not choose to do that? I don't understand why anyone would choose differently.

Researchers always find that people who embrace and express gratitude are happier, healthier and more energetic. So if you want to stay young at heart, be grateful. The more a person is inclined towards gratitude the less likely they are to be stressed, lonely, depressed, anxious or suicidal.

So how do you show gratitude? You can give out compliments, make lists of things you are grateful for, volunteer in your community. Do small, random acts of kindness, and smile. It does not have to be complicated, but it does take a bit of rhythm and routine to share gratitude in your life.

These three small acts when practised daily will have a big impact: handwritten notes, small acts of kindness and daily gratitude check-ins.

GRATITUDE, YOUR CHOICE

You may have heard the saying, 'You can lead a horse to water, but you can't make it drink.' The same goes for the power of gratitude. I can share all the insights in the world in this book but if you don't act on them, they're worth nothing. You will not see results.

That saying always reminds me of when I was around 18 years old. A group of us arranged to go riding and I told the people who managed the horses that I could ride. Yet I had never been on a horse in my life and knew nothing of how to manage one. The horse I was on took off at a gallop and I was so afraid because I did not know how to stop it. I thought I was going to be seriously injured, if not die because it galloped on and on. I was in absolute despair. It galloped and galloped until it got to the water's edge, where it stopped for a drink. It must have been really thirsty and I nerdiered over its head.

This horse wanted the water so much and it was being held back. It was only when it got the freedom, albeit with me on its back, that it galloped to water. So if you're thirsty for gratitude, if you're thirsty for what gratitude can do in your life, gallop to that water's edge and start to action it in your life.

When you reap the rewards of the gratitude and are aware of the results you are getting because you are actioning it, it's the most magnificent thing to experience. It's all well and good to say, 'I am grateful' but that's not action. Those are words. Yes, words are powerful, but words with meaning, with feeling, with purpose are more powerful.

It's your choice and nobody can make it for you. Nobody can do it for you. You can say the words, but if you don't mean them, it's not going to have any effect in your life.

Choosing gratitude is the simplest way to change your life in a short time. It's immediate.

I always choose gratitude. I'm so grateful for the love of my children. I'm so grateful for the opportunities that come my way. I'm so grateful for the beautiful home I'm in. I'm so grateful for my relationships. I'm so grateful for my family.

I'm so grateful that I'm happy and I've chosen to prioritise joy. I'm grateful for lots of things. I could list 100 things right now that I'm grateful for because there's always something to be grateful for even on your darkest day.

Choose gratitude because there's always a glimmer of hope. If you are alive, if you're breathing, that is something to be grateful for.

There's always someone worse off than us. It's about owning our own lives and doing amazing things should we choose to enjoy gratitude.

IF YOU WANT IT, BE GRATEFUL FOR IT NOW

This way of thinking defies everything we have been programmed to believe so you will need to have some faith in the process for it to reach its highest capacity. I can assure you that when you use this correctly it will change your life for the better.

Being grateful for what we have now, both the big and the small things, will bring more of that goodness into our lives and that is wonderful. But what if you could next level the immediate impact in your life to manifest the future of your dreams?

You can! You can do it by being grateful for what you want in the future whilst making yourself subconsciously believe that you have it now. In this way you can trick your mind and subsequently your energy to bring in your heart's desire. I have used this on many occasions and it works so I don't question it, I embrace it.

On many occasions I have observed people building some momentum only to undo the magic in motion by overthinking and talking themselves out of it. WHY?

GRATEFUL PARENTING

Our children are our biggest challenges and our biggest accomplishments. There's no one size fits all when it comes to any child. I'm a mother of six and every one of my children has required a different version of me to parent them.

They come out of the same person and yet they're so different, they don't even look the same. So how do we show gratitude as a parent? Being a parent is one of the most challenging things that you will ever experience in your lifetime and yet one of the most rewarding. I endorse grateful parenting because it always helps me to see the good in any scenario.

When kids play up, I try to see it from a different perspective. Sometimes they need a bit of the tough loving where we say, 'no, that is not okay'. When we're trying to guide our children so that they can be strong enough to make their own decisions rather than control them, that's when wonderful things happen. Every night I'm grateful for each one of my children and I'm grateful for their health. I always say that I'm grateful for their health because when I'm grateful for their health, they're healthy.

My kids rarely get sick and if they are, I just give them so much love. One of my girls has been diagnosed with type one diabetes and that was a big shock to our family. It doesn't mean there's anything wrong, she just has this to deal with and she's going to be fine.

But I'm so grateful she's alive. I'm so grateful that she's making progress. She just has to pause for a moment in life and find her way again and that's okay. We're here to support her. Whenever you're a grateful parent, it gives you the energy that you need to parent.

If you are feeling the stress of being a parent, if you are feeling very heavy and burdened, then you won't have the energy required to be the parent you want to be. It's as simple as that. So that's when it's time to hold up your hand and say I need a break. I certainly do from time to time. We all need a break every now and again.

Even when we try to take the time to be our best version of ourselves, sometimes we're tired or scenarios happen and we end up turning into the parent we don't want to be. And that is life. And that is okay.

You know, all is wonderful.

GRATEFUL RELATIONSHIPS

Be grateful for your relationships. Whether it's your intimate relationship with a partner, your children or with friends, be really grateful for the bonds. Seek out the good in those relationships, focus on that and be grateful for it. Relinquishing expectation can help you to feel gratitude for others.

That's something I've always been good at but you do need to watch out for toxic people who are there to take advantage of that. It's interesting to observe relationships in action. You can have positive and negative thoughts around a relationship and that will have an impact on the relationship. Focus on the relationship negatively and you will have a negative experience of it. Focus on it positively and you will have a more positive experience of it.

I know from experience that no matter how strong your mind is, when your heart is involved, it can be tough or so wonderful. It's about getting that balance right and knowing who energises you and who's worth the effort. You need to choose that for you. No metaphysical book or anybody else can do that for you. That is your responsibility.

You choose who you want to have around you, who you want to energise you, or if you do choose someone that maybe hangs out in the negative, just pray that you rub off on them a little bit. But if they're toxic, no matter how much positive energy you pump into that person, they are never going to fill you up, they're never going to energise you. It is only ever going to be a one-way scenario and they're going to be an energy vampire. They're going to take the energy from you and they're not going to share it around. That's not how the universe works so it's important for us to have active relationships with people.

We can be connected to someone in our family, or to someone who isn't the best person in the world, but that doesn't mean we are actively in a relationship with them. We might only see them at a birthday or a wedding or casually. But if you are actively connecting and having a relationship with someone, whether it is intimate, or with your children, your family or in a friendship, if it's an active relationship that is toxic it will take away from you. If it's an active relationship that involves two-way giving, there's love in it, and it's energising. So it's up to you.

But be grateful for all relationships, because through their intricacies they all help us to grow. Some toughen us up, some soften us down. What is important is to always keep the love in your heart unshielded, because nothing should ever make you shield your heart. The love always needs to be active, always needs to be open, always needs to be pouring into someone or something.

And when you're being grateful for the relationships you have, focus on those that deserve your love. Pour into them and allow them to pour into you and wait to see the difference in your life.

HAPPY DANCE WITH GRATITUDE FOR NEXT LEVEL IMPACT

Goodness me. When something happens that you've been waiting or hoping for, something on your bucket list, stop and smell the roses because if you don't, you're missing out on a happy dance moment. If you don't action an inspired thought in the moment of it, it goes and in the same way, if you don't happy dance in a happy dance moment, it passes. So don't let it pass. Grab it, celebrate it.

Let the world know. Let that ball of energy come from deep within you, from every atom in your body. Let it beam from you, that energetic pulsation that emits from your body. It is an amazing magnet that attracts more of it to you. I have had these moments often. One of the biggest years of happy dance moments for me was 2020 yet the rest of the world was going through a pandemic. I didn't feel guilt because I thought, well, our world needs more people having happy dance moments so we can start to fix and heal it. The world was gripped by the energy that surrounds fear around health. The pandemic was real, people were dying and it was horrendous and so many people were affected by it.

And yet here I was in my little bubble in Perth, Western Australia, where we had closed borders and less exposure to the pandemic. I felt so much empathy for people elsewhere, but I knew the world needed us to embrace what was happening. For me on a personal level it was important to be able to emit happy dance moments, to show that life was still happening, to say, 'Don't get entrenched in the news.'

From a metaphysics perspective, the mind comes before the body and your body reacts to what your mind is thinking. The mind is powerful and when it is overwhelmed with unhealthy thoughts, guess what? You become unhealthy. And when you become unhealthy, overwhelmed, tired or rundown, living at a low vibration, it hits you like a rocket.

What the world needs is for us to have our happy dance moments with deep gratitude for what's happening and what we are making happen in the world. We do that by celebrating the wins, sharing those wins with people so that they can get the vibe and go, 'Wow, world, things are still happening for people. There's hope, there's a glimmer.' I'm not sharing to rub it in your face. I'm sharing so that you can see there are still good things happening for good people.

So happy dance with gratitude for next level impact, because you have to, because the world needs you to, because your community needs you to, because your family needs you to, because you need you to, too.

That energy is healing energy. That energy is manifesting energy. That energy makes a difference. And it is not selfish. It is fruitful, it is energising and it is very important.

GRATITUDE IN BUSINESS

I have always loved the concept of being grateful in business. Gratitude is deemed to be something for our personal not professional life, but I know from experience that when you bring gratitude into the workplace it has great results.

If you are in business or are planning to launch a business venture, incorporate gratitude in all the connections you make. It lets people know that you acknowledge and appreciate what they have done for you.

It's so important that we take time to be grateful in our business, and it needs to become second nature. Not that we need to bombard people with it, but just taking a moment to send a gift, or write an email that isn't rushed but written with more connection makes a difference. Build a rapport with the people you do business with in an authentic, genuine way.

You're not just looking for the money. You are wanting to work with the person and you want to get to know them. Everybody's different. I'm in publishing and one of the things I love about my business is getting to know my authors. There's a lot of work in publishing and it can be stressful at times for some people because of the journey they're on. I always make time to go on the journey with them and it's always amazing.

Taking a moment to be grateful and show gratitude in our actions as well as our words makes people feel valued when you are doing business with them. They're not just a number. That's the focus in my business because I genuinely love connecting with the people whose journey I'm sharing. There will always be some people who are your people and some people who aren't, and that's okay. But when you do go on the journey with someone, it makes good business sense to keep that integrity with you, to be grateful and to really connect.

I get called into business arenas now to speak on the Power of Knowing, which is one of my seven life principles. When you know how to *know*, you can make decisions with unwavering faith that where you're going is the right direction. It saves you time, energy and mistakes. It's the same with gratitude. You can use gratitude as a tool to bring on a new client and if they push it away or react to it badly, then they are not your client. You do not want to take them on board.

Perhaps they're simply not used to it yet. But if someone has a real issue with you being grateful, then they're going to have an issue with a lot of other things on the journey with your service so it'll end up costing you energetically and probably financially by the end of your contract with them. I always start with gratitude and see how they react to it, and then I use it as a kind of gauging tool as to whether they are my ideal client or not. My ideal clients are able to appreciate gratitude because they understand the value in it, they understand I'm going to do my best for them and they are grateful in return, which means I want to do more for them.

That's the way the universe works and anyone who's resistant to that is resistant to the process of evolution, of things happening, so there are going to be a lot more blocks. Gratitude can be a really good gauging tool when bringing on clients. Try it!

BEING GRATEFUL WHEN
YOU DON'T FEEL IT

Being grateful even for the hard lessons is a tough one, it really is.

The hard lessons weigh heavy on our hearts. They force us to go inward. They're uncomfortable. They bring us out of ourselves because what we thought to be is not the case. That's a tough lesson to learn, especially if you've invested a lot of emotional energy in making something happen.

So how do we change our perspective from shame, anger, pain, sadness, all of those darker emotions? How do we salvage what we can, and have a positive reaction to these tough times? Gratitude is the way out. In *The Visitor* I used a quote at the beginning that I did not know at the time would be the essence of that book.

'From every negative situation, there is the potential for a positive outcome.'

If you are not aligned with your intentions and goals, with your highest potential, the universe will halt you in your tracks every now and again to make you stop and re-evaluate, reassess and get some clarity. Sometimes it can be a big shock to the system. Your nervous system physically gets shocked, and you have to pause and process what's happened. It's not a time for action.

Please note that. It's not a time for action. But no matter how dark any day is, there's always something to be grateful for.

So find it. Let it shine through. Let it carry you through, and let something amazing come from that.

GRATITUDE AFFIRMATIONS

It pays huge dividends to choose gratitude. The energy in your atoms will be happier and your results will speak for themselves!

Gratitude helps you instantly rewire old thinking patterns. It can be easily embraced with a simple shift in perspective.

On the next page I have compiled 20 common gratitudes. I would love for you to add 10 more.

1. *I am grateful for the life I have.*

2. *I am grateful that I have choices.*

3. *I am grateful to be able to give and receive unconditional love.*

4. *I am grateful for self-love.*

5. *I am grateful for my friends.*

6. *I am grateful for all the opportunities that come my way.*

7. *I am grateful for inspired thoughts and actions.*

8. *I am grateful for my personal freedom.*

9. *I am grateful that I can make a difference in this world.*

10. *I am grateful for my family.*

11. *I am grateful for my occupation.*

12. *I am grateful for laughter.*

13. *I am grateful for my interests.*

14. *I am grateful for my home.*

15. *I am grateful for the food I eat.*

16. *I am grateful for my daily walk.*

17. *I am grateful that I am me.*

18. *I am grateful for time.*

19. *I am grateful when someone takes a moment to connect.*

20. *I am grateful for beautiful places and experiences.*

Add 10 things that you can be grateful for in your life:

1.

2.

3.

4.

5.

6.

7.

8.

9.

10.

LOVE-FUELLED GRATITUDE

One thing I've noticed that sets me and other super manifestors out from the pack is that we embrace love. There is an unlimited supply of love within us all; in fact the more we use love, the more love grows!

Please read this line below until it is ingrained inside you.

When you are grateful with all your heart it is a super fuel!

I know this because I have not only observed it, I have actioned it on many occasions. Not everyone has the ability to open their heart freely. Kids do it but as we become adults, we become distrustful and damaged because of past experiences.

Being grateful with all of your heart becomes a super fuel and it means that you work as one with the universe because the universe *is* love. When we begin to trust and have faith that it works solely for us, and that the energy created through love teamed with the energy of gratitude because gratitude is love, it is a super fuel for success. It will deliver whatever you channel the energy on, so be sure to remain mindful of your intentions around that.

I'm going to share with you a secret hack here, one that super manifestors understand implicitly. Learn to pour love and gratitude into what you want but don't already have and it will come to you. Sit in the essence of feeling that you have it right now for a few minutes a day, then watch and wait as it finds its way to you. You will know when you need to action the steps but my goodness, wait till you see how fast it comes your way when you pair love and gratitude together and trust in the process.

The world is your oyster, there is nothing you cannot achieve. Keep it simple. Too often we make it complicated. You need to feel unconditional love and have total faith in your ability to manifest. Be grateful for what it feels like to have the thing that you want in your future. Sit in the essence of what that would be like and the best way to do that is in visualisation. Close your eyes and just sit with it, because if we can create it in our mind, we can create it in our reality.

You need to know what you want and be open to feeling what it is like to receive it. Pump loving energy and gratitude into that moment because not only is it in your head it's in your heart. Once you bring it through your head and heart it starts to vibrate through your body, and it becomes real in the senses before you even have it in your hands or experience it in reality. It actually becomes real in that moment of manifestation. It is the most powerful process in the whole of existence and when you have learned the power of love-fuelled gratitude you will never manifest any other way.

THE GRATITUDE JOYRIDE

When we are joyful, we raise our vibration and that's contagious. Others can benefit from our energy. It energises them as well, so it has a ripple effect.

I remember a time when I chose joy. I used to write for a magazine called *Universal Mind*. I think I had four children at the time and may have been pregnant with my fifth. However, I went to visit the magazine owner, who didn't live far from me. She invited me over and it was very serendipitous how she started finding my writings and using them in her magazines.

But that's another story. What I wanted to share with you was that she said she wanted to read for me. I'm always open to that so she did a reading using numerology and said, 'Where you are on your life path, you're about to go into a joyride setting. And when that happens, it's just going to be like you're riding the waves like a dolphin.'

'Wow,' I said. 'Cool.'

'No,' she said. 'You don't understand how big it's going to get, but just keep riding the waves, having the fun, enjoying the love of your children because that's what will energise you. And just do it your way. Don't worry about anybody else. Just keep doing what you love and enjoy, and you'll have so much success. It's as if you're just going to be riding the waves. It's big dolphins. That's what I see.'

I've been doing this now for about ten years so in numerology terms I'm probably back full circle on that cycle, which is interesting. One thing I've observed is that over those past ten years I have been on many joyrides. And when you are energised and success is happening and everything is so free flowing and fun, it's energising, it really and truly is.

It also requires you to be very activated all the time. You don't feel tired because you're running on adrenaline. It's fun. I've been on those kinds of life joyrides for six months at a time.

But one thing I'm always mindful of is to really enjoy the power of the pause. When there's a lull and maybe I've planted another seed of intention, I've done what I can to make that happen and it's a quiet period, I usually distract myself with something else. But it's also important to understand that a big part of the process of manifesting is to embrace that down time so that you can replenish those energy fields within you that will fuel the next part of the cycle. We need to step back and cuddle our kids again just to make sure we have that beautiful blend because otherwise we will run out of the joyride rocket fuel.

Love is one of the biggest super fuels for manifesting. You don't want to burn out when you're on a joyride, you want to enjoy every moment of it so it's important to keep your cup full. Our job is to keep moving forward, keep working towards things that bring us joy, that we see in front of us. Just keep taking that next step. Do not think of the big picture. We know the essence of what we want so it is not our job to think of the big picture because that will overwhelm us. All the things that need to happen to get from here to there will overwhelm you and you will run a mile. You'll feel it as overwhelming struggle and you will bail out.

Before any breakthrough there's always a struggle but when you take it step by step you've walked a mile before you realise it's an important milestone. One of your duties when it comes to manifesting, or going on the journey to receiving or whatever you want to call it, is to keep your cup full, because when the joyride comes, you're going to need that energy. You're going to need that cup full and you're going to need reserves for your family. You will also need reserves for other things that you will not have full focus on, so that will enable you to enjoy the rewards that you reap. You won't feel like you've compromised on your values because you've got this beautiful blend of energy, and anyone who loves you will want to see you happy once you keep the lines of communication open and say, 'This is really important, this is a goal that I've been working really hard towards, we'll all reap the benefits of it.'

When that joyride comes, you know it. You have to allow yourself to embrace it and reap the rewards from it because that is high vibe contagious. Everyone will want a piece of that and you have to maximise on that so you can continue to inspire others. Personal development and peak performance pioneer Jack Canfield says one of mistakes made by the great leaders of the past is that they never empowered others with their wisdoms. They kept them to themselves. And that is one of the big things that's wrong with the world. People are keeping things to themselves and they should be sharing with each other. Sharing is how we grow. There's enough for everybody.

In fact, if we're all raising the vibration of the world, the world is going to be a great place for us all, we're all going to benefit. So embrace the joyride, harness the joy. Keep the cup full and pour into those around you.

BEING THE CHANGE – THE WORLD NEEDS MORE GRATITUDE

Imagine a world led by gratitude. Leaders who embrace what it means to appreciate the efforts of others. I look back on many scenarios in history and see that well intentioned actions were often misread, and had the immediate reaction been one of appreciation rather than retaliation it may have changed the course of history. It's not too late to change our reactions to things on a personal and professional level.

Remember it's a universal law! Every action attracts an equal reaction so it's important to be mindful of how we react to things, how we act and what our intentions are, but to also be mindful of what's around others. I really feel the essence of that, and to be the change we need to be more grateful and kind to each other in the world. When we react and act through the essence of gratitude and kindness, we will see a significant difference in world interactions and connections.

If someone is well intentioned but what they do is wrongly perceived, the reaction to it is totally misaligned to their intention. It's an emotionally fuelled reaction and that's a recipe for disaster. Consider options and count to five before you react, especially if it's going to be an emotional reaction. You could be responding to a trigger from the past. It's just as important to be mindful of people's intentions around their actions as well as your reactions to them. When we do that, especially in leadership, but even on a day-to-day personal level with our families and the people we meet, it will make a positive difference.

Where parenting is concerned, a child is coming from a

different place of knowledge, awareness and wisdom. They haven't experienced a lot of life challenges and they have a lot to learn. When they react with a tantrum or in an unexpected way, our reaction is important because they learn from us. We're the adults and in their eyes, we're supposed to have it all together. They're going to learn from our reactions, not from our words so how we act needs to be aligned with what we say.

Be mindful of that also around your connections with adults and understand that people have different levels of emotional intelligence or could be responding to a trigger from a past life that has nothing to do with you. You may just be a catalyst to reaction for somebody who needs to deal with an issue. We don't have to walk around on eggshells but we do need to be mindfully aware because usually energetically we can pick up on this. Especially if you're an open-hearted person and you're dealing with someone who doesn't embrace open-hearted people.

You can bring out the best and the worst in people. Be mindful and accepting of that and don't take too much on board personally because it's not always personal. Be the change that you want to see in the world. Spread more gratitude and kindness wherever you go and we will all see the difference that makes.

GRATITUDE AND HEALTH

Be mindful of your own health journey. Know what that is for you. Know that miracles do happen. Know that you can heal.

There are many cases of hospitals and doctors making people believe they are incurable, and they lose hope. But when you have hope, when you have faith, belief and knowledge that your mind can help you to heal, having a happy heart and a positive attitude can help you defy all odds. That's a superpower. I want to share with you a little story about my dad. I love my dad. He's an amazing man.

A few years after we moved to Australia, he had two strokes, one after the other, a few months apart. And I never felt the distance so much in my life. But one of the things that surprised and shocked me more than anything was that he was so determined and so forward focused and would not accept anything else but that he was going to get better. Within a year he was on an aeroplane to Australia to see me because I just had another child.

He had a walking stick, but he still came and he never let himself be defeated. A year or two later, he had a CT scan of his brain to check the stroke damage and to our shock, his brain was fully healed. Compare that with my grandfather, who was quite happy to believe what the doctor said. After he had a stroke, he just sat in his chair all day. He'd light a fire and sit there in the kitchen or the living room and that was all I ever knew of my granddad.

It's interesting when I compare the two. There's no way my dad would accept that as his destiny. Some people are happy to accept a diagnosis, have an easier life and not take any risks. Had I not taken a risk and become pregnant again after a miscarriage, I would never have had any more children for fear of losing one. My dad could have given in to the fear of having another stroke and enjoyed less of a life. He's getting older, but he's not in any way held back because of what happened.

When we focus on optimum health, we achieve optimum health. So give your brain the gift of that. Visualise yourself healthy. Should you come down with an ailment, know that it's for a reason. Discover what that is for you. If something keeps coming up, you need to address it. Knowing that is so important.

Be grateful for your health, the health you have now. If you don't have your optimum health now, be grateful for optimum health in your future, because when you do that, you are manifesting a healthier future. And do we not all want that?

Don't just accept that you're getting older. Don't just accept that you're getting sicker. Know that whatever you accept in your mind is what you will experience. So don't just accept it. Defy it.

Aim higher. Know that miracles happen because if you believe in yourself and others believe in you, nothing is impossible. Remember the power that's in your mind and in your heart and in every atom of your being to regenerate, to heal. We are forever healing all the time.

Embrace the healing potential that you have. Activate the healing potential that you have. Supercharge the healing potential that you have in your life. And wait till you see the results.

Be grateful for your health now. In the future you will feel the benefits.

GRATEFUL CREATIVITY

I have been through a few lulls in creativity. Sometimes I'm really energetically buzzing but creatively, the juices don't flow. And by creativity I don't just mean my writing, I'm also talking about the manifesting, that free-flowing energy where things happen.

If you're a business owner or if you're trying to achieve something in your life, it's really important to have that energetic flow. It truly is. But you won't have it 100% of the time, I don't believe anybody does. It depends on the circumstances. When we are embracing those things and allowing them to be in flow, then it's amazing what can happen.

Right now, I am in the most beautiful creative energy. There are books pouring out of me, left, right and centre. I've been creative with projects and business ideas and my authors are loving it. But it's hard to sustain that all of the time and to be authentic because creativity is a gift, it's a flow, it's magic. And to be able to have it is an honour, because it's divine creativity.

It's so special. There are golden nuggets that come through it, there are messages to help other people. All of those golden essence things in life come through creative energy, even your finances. If you want to earn extra money, if you want to manifest money, you need creative energy to do that. That's why it's important to be grateful for creative energy, so that you have more of it. Being able to identify it, embrace it and harness it is so important in life when you have things you want to achieve.

Creative energy flourishes beautifully in simplicity, in that lovely energy of joy and happiness. Creative energy comes when you have had enough sleep, because if your brain is tired, it's not going to flare.

A lot of people have had the stuffing knocked out of their creative energy following COVID due to foggy brain and exhaustion. 'Long COVID' has been likened to chronic fatigue and it's hard for creative juices to flow when you're in survival mode.

Creativity flourishes when there's a beautiful balance in your soul of happiness, of curiosity, just the sense of being. That's when creativity flows beautifully. So be grateful for it when you have it, because it is worth its weight in gold. Be grateful for it, identify it and really utilise it. Make room for that magic in your life, and you will reap the rewards.

My top tips for embracing and ensuring that you have the maximum amount of creative energy in your life are:

- Remain high vibrational so that you're connected to the Divine, because creative energy is a divine source.
- Get enough sleep.
- Get up early so that you can tap into the creative source, especially if there are goals you want to achieve in business or in life.
- Understand that you're not going to be creative all the time, and that's okay. Don't fear that lull, but do everything you can to nurture the environment for creativity to flourish.
- Love life and it will love you back.

THE NO-FEAR APPROACH TO GRATITUDE

Fear stops any dream in its tracks so it's really important that we have a no-fear approach to gratitude. When we're filled with gratitude, our hearts are open, we're free-flowing, we are embracing the potential of every moment, we're grateful for what we've received and for what we're going to receive. And we can't have any fear around it so when manifesting we have to have trust in the process.

So set the intention, action the inspired thoughts and opportunities, and have no fear around saying yes. Be grateful before, during and after that process, and have no fear that it's all coming together. It is so important to have no fear attached to it because fear will pull any high vibrational energy right down. Fear is a human instinct that is there to protect us but when we are manifesting and wanting to make dreams come true, that road can be a little unsettling.

There's always a struggle before a breakthrough so when we meet challenges or big opportunities come our way, fear always steps up first to allow us the gift of processing and releasing any inhibitions we have around it. It's important that this comes at the beginning, because there's no point in it coming at the end. When any of my authors start to get inhibitions after they have sent me their book, and fear sets in, I always say, 'Just honour it and acknowledge it, but move through it.'

It's good to have the fear at the beginning of the process because then when your book is being released and put out into the world, you've already dealt with that, you're already a step ahead. Fear is not your enemy. Fear is there to help you process and move through and honour and acknowledge any inhibitions that may come up around an experience.

There are all different scenarios but I like to use the author one as a good example. Authors will be grateful that they've written a book, but when the book is written and they have started to move into the publishing process, then they realise that this book is going to be out in the world. That can bring up feelings of fear but they're thinking too far ahead.

It's important to acknowledge the fear because when you acknowledge it, you're giving it energy and moving past it so that it doesn't take up any more of your energy. You can move forward with faith and courage to make that goal happen. So honour and feel the fear and do what you want to do anyway.

Whenever you are manifesting or whenever anything is happening, be grateful. Gratitude will get you through those moments of fear. Fear does start to peek through but you don't want to suppress it, you don't want to push it down.

You want to honour it and release it and move on from it. *Hi, fear, how are you going? I see you wearing your ugly head. It's all right, it's cool. I'm fine. Here, I've got this.*

And the fear will leave you. *All right. She seems cool. She seems so fierce in the process, we'll trust her.*

My three top tips for having a no-fear approach to manifesting

- Embrace gratitude. Pour positive energy into anything that you're doing and it will help you to stay high vibrational so that you can move past fear.
- Don't suppress the fear. Acknowledge it, move through it and honour it.

- Understand that fear has its place. For many people, fear is part of the process, and understanding and realising that is important, but it doesn't have to be the roadblock that it is. Don't let it pull you down too much.

The Freedom
in Forgiveness

Forgiving others is not a gift to them,
it is a gift to ourselves.

ONE-SIDED FORGIVENESS

What do we do in the scenario when we are seeking forgiveness from someone who is not willing to give it? How do we move on from the energy of maybe they want revenge? Maybe they hold so much resentment for us that we're not going to receive forgiveness. It's not good to think about, and I understand that.

If you are truly sorry and someone chooses not to forgive, that's on them, not on you. So if you have sought forgiveness and it hasn't been received, well, then so be it. If that's not totally comfortable for you, I do have an alternative solution, which is to tap into the energy of that person. Either when you're in a quiet state of mind, maybe in a meditative state, or in a pause moment where you're just sitting and being, and where you really think about that person, connect into their energy and internally say, 'I'm sorry'.

And whether they will want to accept it is not up to them. They will have to, because energetically they will receive it if they're not absolutely blocking it out. So be in a quiet space, take a moment to go into connecting with their energy. And if you're struggling with that, you can come over to my website where you will find *Mindful Moments*. Click on the tab and you can listen to it. It'll get you into the state of mind required to connect with their energy.

So it's important to take that moment to tap into their energy. You can also use that tapping into their energy mindful moment to let someone know that you love them, because people who are not closed to emotion are receptive of energetic vibrations.

I've done this a lot, and in my experience, it has a positive effect when you use it for good. Just take a moment to tap into their energy. They don't have to be really receptive. As long as they aren't a brick wall to energetic flow, they will feel benefits. The impact will differ from person to person. It depends on the connection you have with them.

It doesn't matter how much physical difference there is between you when you tap into their energy with all of your heart and ask for forgiveness. Love is the super fuel here. It will bring any transmitted energy there faster. You will be coming into their energy field and they will subconsciously know it. It's bizarre how it works, but when it's done for good, for healing and forgiveness and for love, it's a beautiful thing.

Then you have to accept, and allow yourself to feel, the benefits of being untied from the need to seek forgiveness. It may feel uncomfortable if you come face to face with this person again at various times in your life, but you will know you have made that energetic connection and are untied from the obligation for forgiveness.

One thing you cannot do in this life is control somebody else's actions, especially if they have their own lessons to learn. You can only do your utmost to seek forgiveness if it is your fault, and then let it go.

It's a really important exercise, short but powerful, so it's worth doing. It's really worth treasuring.

FORGIVE AND FORGET?

I perceive myself as a forgiving person who processes experiences without holding onto negativity and moves on. Yet I have struggled with the general expectation that once we forgive, everything will return to the way it was in our relationships with each other.

Relationships are constantly evolving and when there is a situation that requires forgiveness, obviously things are not going to be the same as they were. The relationship is coming from a different space.

My husband and I have been together for twenty-one years and some serious things have happened between us that have required a high level of forgiveness. Obviously, that changes the relationship because trust is affected. There's also some shame to deal with, a lot of grief energy, and that deep heart-wrenching sense of **what was, will never be again**. All of those things! And as much as you can heal your heart and forgive and move on, the incidents or scenarios still change you because they all are part of your memories, tattooed into your future self, so it's evolutionary.

After going through a forgiveness process with somebody, there's no way in the world that your relationship will be the same as it was beforehand. Yes, there may be an expectation of 'forgive and forget', but I think it's more 'forgive and move on', because you can't forget what has happened. It's part of your memory bank.

And why would you want to forget? Every experience has led to us becoming the person we are today. Everything that has happened in our life, whether it was last year or a decade ago, has contributed to who we are and how we evolve. It's important for us to honour that and to allow ourselves the freedom of accepting that things have happened and that's OK.

The new you with the value lessons that you have learnt because of what you've experienced may change your relationships with others and they may not like that. You may miss and grieve for the relationship you had before but one thing is certain: you can't go backwards. You can only move forwards; and if you move forwards with love and with a positive attitude, then you will honour the lesson from whatever you needed to forgive. You will free yourself from any negative energy pulling you back, so you can move on and continue moving forward.

When we're in divine energy, we move on and free ourselves from these experiences, but learn the lesson from them.

If you're working with the universal laws, carrying the burden of whatever has happened to you or feeling you have been wronged is not what you need. You need to forgive and move on. But as for the forgetting, I believe that happens after the 'wounds' have healed. Forgiving occurs first and forgetting follows once healing has taken place.

When you've done the healing, the emotion around what happened is neutral. The experience is just something that's part of who you are now. It is more important to heal around the scenario than to forget it.

You have to find the courage to work through the situation, talk about it, maybe seek counselling. That's really important because it isn't healthy to suppress what's happened in an attempt to make it go away. That kind of suppression can lead to a range of ailments and even serious diseases. It's not OK to sweep the whole thing under the carpet and ignore it. Don't bury it deep inside yourself. People are becoming ill because they are suppressing things that need to be addressed. Have the courage to show up for yourself and deal with it.

Have the courage. I need to learn this as well. I need to practise this more in my life, but at least I've identified it. There's nothing worse than holding the shame or trauma of something within you that is not yours to hold. Maybe the person doesn't understand how their behaviour or actions affected you, so you need to tell them so they can learn. If they do it again when they're informed of the effect on you, and it's with malice, it's up to you how you respond.

Yes, these situations can be traumatic for us. 'I didn't sign up for this,' you think, or 'Wow! I didn't see that coming,' and it shakes your nervous system. When that happens, we go into survival mode. We try to process the experience. To understand why it triggered us. You do need to process it, especially if it's been traumatic for you.

Others may ask, 'What's wrong with you? Why are you so reactive to that?' Whereas that's not the case. The fact is that you have something important to process to understand yourself.

Take the time to understand, set your boundaries, have the necessary conversations. Conversations are powerful.

Write down what's happened. Once you do that it becomes something tangible to work with. Write the person a letter to get it out of your system.

You can forgive, and you can forget... after the healing has taken place.

FORGIVENESS AND MONEY

You might not think forgiveness and money would go hand in hand, however it is important to consider them in relation to each other. Money is energy according to the universal laws and any blocks you have around it are because of your energy around it.

Therefore, it's important that you embrace forgiveness when it comes to money. That can be forgiveness in the sense of your own financial habits and spending, or it can be forgiveness for how you earn or receive money from others. There has to be forgiveness around every aspect of money. Your energy around it needs to be clear from guilt, shame, any sense of being unworthy, or feeling like a charity case.

What I always suggest is that you forgive yourself all of that, along with any limiting beliefs from childhood. Many people hold onto shame that is not theirs and not understanding how the universal laws work, they live in poverty.

Release yourself from that energy and gravitate instead into gratitude. There is abundance in gratitude. When we're grateful for what we have, we will have more to be grateful for.

Our world needs more good people earning good money so that more good things will happen on this planet. Let me repeat that: We need more good people earning good money so that good things can happen in the work we do.

Faith and forgiveness are imperative when it comes to money.

Our mindset sets the scene, it's the launch pad and the landing pad, that's why forgiveness is important.

Forgive yourself and others if you have money blocks. Love what you have, live for what you love, and really enjoy the life that you have with confidence, knowing that you are deserving of it all.

Money that comes from bad energy will only bring unpleasant results. It's important to be true to your values when it comes to calling in money. If you hold any shame or guilt around it, go into forgiveness. Release the shame and guilt and move into gratitude as quickly as you can.

Whenever we manoeuvre and manipulate life aligned with our values, then we're all good. Sometimes there's a grey area. It's OK to get lost in the shadow sometimes. Allow your energy to shift and realign with your values. Learn from it, and know you are not a bad person if you do good things. Forgiveness is imperative in any aspect of manifesting, especially when it comes to money.

It's important to understand that there will always be feasts and famines in life. There will be times where I have very successful businesses and times when cash flow is low. When cash flow is high, we do good things and good work. And when it's low, we do the work to get the cash flow high again. It's all ebbs and flows, the ebbs and flows of life. You need to focus, readjust, realign and recalibrate, and when done with the right intentions, it will bring you the most epic journey.

You can't worry when money becomes scarce, because if you focus on that, the money will become scarcer. Focus on abundance and you will have more. It's as simple as that.

So release yourself from any shame surrounding money, whether it's money coming in or money going out. Release yourself, forgive yourself, forgive others and don't hold on to it. How do I know? Because I do it.

Be grateful for every bill you pay, that you've had the money to pay it, because many people don't, and forgive when needed.

FORGIVENESS AND THE
WALK AWAY METHOD

We're not going to be everyone's cup of tea. We're going to rub some people up the wrong way just by simply being us, no matter how well intentioned we are. There will be those who are jealous, or misunderstand our actions and come to their own conclusions.

Recently I've started to navigate a new direction in a certain part of my journey.

I began to put some energy into authorship again. Obviously, I started this journey as an author, but I went into publishing to serve and to help people. For ten years I've been on a quest, building a brand and a publishing empire, and investing very heavily to create a platform for authors to shine and create opportunities. Authorship is my own personal endeavour, and I know through my words I actually help people, which makes my heart sing.

Writing this book and putting energy into my authorship brought a lot of issues to the surface that required forgiveness. In situations like this, when you start to transition, some of the people in your life will behave towards you in a way that catches you off guard. This happened to me and it was disappointing, but I had to understand where these people were in their lives. Also, I know that everything happens for a reason. It's always for the greater good, though it doesn't feel like it at the time and can be quite unsettling. It does lead you to act and create the space for the magic of what it is that you're truly wanting to manifest into your life. I realised space was actually being cleared for me to allow my authorship to come through.

All of those things have to be considered so that I can forgive and let go with love. Everything done in love is done with the best intention and I am very blessed to have no emotion connected to this process, for that's where anger can come in. Anger can pull you down, lead to depression, or hold you back from moving forward.

So, I don't ignore what's happened, I process it. In some cases, I have a conversation with the person involved, but as soon as that happens, I automatically energetically disconnect with them. They've lost my goodwill, but I let them go with love.

Sometimes we are only in people's lives for a season, so we have to acknowledge that, respect them and their journey, and also respect our own journey. It's important to have the courage to let go with love when necessary and move on. This doesn't have to be a harrowing experience, it can just be a case of accepting, 'it's OK.' In that, there's peace.

A special gift of room for magic is created through the ability to let go of the energetic ties that hold you back, and forgiveness is a big part of that. Honour that, allow it to be, and be grateful to the Universe. Just be aware while you're reading and processing this forgiveness book that issues will come to the surface. They're not there to make you feel uncomfortable and pull you down, they're actually there to free you and make room for magic.

So identify that, honour that, and enjoy it.

FORGIVENESS AND HAPPINESS

Most people strive for happiness in life and are on a quest to achieve it. Yet happiness is something you can have right now, all that's required is a change in perspective. But you cannot have true happiness if you do not learn how to forgive and are holding onto past hurts.

When you're happy, you smile and you feel this physically in your heart, it energetically emits the most beautiful energy from you.

Why would we not choose happiness?

Happiness is love of self and love of life. If you love yourself and you want to love your life, you need to increase forgiveness.

From a universal perspective, I don't believe forgiveness is a gift to the other person. It's a gift to yourself. We are often taught from childhood to forgive the person and forget what happened. That's not it. We're supposed to process the incident, be grateful for the lesson and move on from it.

To truly be happy, ensure that you forgive on your terms, understanding that doing so has freed you to manifest more beautiful things in your life.

If the forgiveness is forced or being offered under a sense of obligation, it actually creates resentment. And nobody's worth the energy that takes from you. They really aren't.

Not everyone is evolved to the same level. Their behaviour may come from ignorance, trauma, or any number of scenarios. So that's why we need to learn to forgive and understand that everyone comes from a different perspective. Once you allow the grace of a situation to unfold, that's when the magic happens.

I love my life. I love the energy. But I deal every day with things I have to forgive, we all do. And some things are harder than others. Sometimes I find myself talking ill of somebody, and I catch myself because the energy around that is not productive, or it's not serving me well.

Why would I give it energy when it's detracting from my experience of life?

I take a moment to pause, to recalibrate, to come to the situation from a different angle.

Choose happiness always. Happiness is a choice. It's not a destination. It's a choice we make every day, something we invest in energetically.

Smile with every muscle in your face. Smile in your heart. This heals things that you could never even comprehend. Your atoms are happy when you're smiling.

When you're happy, you feel better and that means everyone around you benefits. It makes sense to prioritise happiness. Happiness is love of self. And forgiveness is where happiness resides.

Many people wonder why they can't be happy. It's because they need to forgive and let go of whatever it is they are holding onto.

But do it your way. Do it in your own style.

You might even enjoy the process. Imagine that.

So, if you want to live the highest vibration of happiness, choose to forgive. It's never too late to forgive.

FORGIVENESS AND THE FREEDOM TO LOVE

Some of us take for granted what others dream of in their lives. The freedom to love with your heart and to choose your own partner is unfortunately not acceptable all over the world. However, it is something that you can work towards. Love is something that captures us at different times of our lives. Falling in love and choosing a partner for life is a big deal. But if we overthink it, it intrudes on the actual freedom of love.

When we commit to the journey with someone, it's like the journey of intention because we have to commit to it with all of our heart. Go on the journey, there will be ups and downs and ins and outs. Things will always be happening within those times of peace and harmony. To be in love, to be in that safe, magical feeling of being loved, is special.

Most people would rather have loved than to not have known love at all. Love always requires forgiveness. I've talked many times about how I find my relationship very challenging. I've had to forgive a lot. I know I'm not alone in that. And in my relationship, there have also definitely been times when I have needed to be forgiven.

Forgiveness is all part of loving someone, whether it's a partner, a family member, or a friend. It's always easier to forgive something that's happened unintentionally or through circumstances, but when someone goes out of their way to hurt you, that's much harder to forgive. I struggle in those instances because I can allow myself to forgive and find the freedom in that, but I don't tend to forget.

So those things can build up. I tend to see in others that inability to forget when things are done intentionally. There's always the moral question, do we stay friends, or remain in a marriage or relationship with someone who has intentionally hurt us?

My heart says no. Yet I have stayed in my relationship and tried to navigate the amicable line and the forgiveness line there. It is tough and it takes the magic out of love, but empathy comes in, and remembering the vows I made.

Marriage is for better or for worse, for richer or for poorer, in sickness and in health, which is a tough gig to navigate, especially in this age, when a lot of us are used to our freedoms and our choices. When someone intentionally hurts us, we usually block them out. We rid ourselves of their toxic behaviour. I'm not in the worst scenario. Some people are trapped in terrible marriages or relationships or forced to marry people they don't love.

I still have freedom of choice. I still can choose to forgive and to forget. Maybe I could have made different choices. We don't always make choices that are aligned with our higher good. But I do try, and I see so many other people trying as well, so what I choose is the freedom to love. It's always magical.

Try to get back to that core, that magic, that glow, that lights you up. And when you can do that, it helps you find your way. If you can't reconnect with that and there's lots of forgiving to do, it's up to you to decide whether that's worth it for you or not. Joy and happiness should be a priority when you choose to live a life at a higher vibration.

So shield yourself from other people's behaviour and you can still have the life of your dreams, should you choose to.

One of my top tips for protecting yourself is embracing the feeling of love. Try to harness that energy of when you first fell in love. Capture the essence of it in your heart, have that feeling in your memory bank so you can access it. It will supercharge anything you pour it into.

If you want money and you sit with a vision of yourself with all the money in the world and how that feels; and if you can inject it with some of that lustful loving energy, that leads to powerful manifesting.

If you want to find love or have had it and lost it, then sit in a visualisation of what it would be like to be so in love and be so loved in return. Love is not one-sided, it's an interaction between two people. So sit in the energy of how that would be, and infuse it with that super- charged feeling. If you haven't had the joy or the honour of knowing what love is, think of a child. Think of something that you love, something that just lights you up, because surely there's something that brings you joy. Go there.

Here are some more tips for shielding yourself from emotions that are not high vibrational when you're going through a tough time in love or any other aspect of your life.

Detach yourself from the scenario emotionally.

Don't be reactive, but don't be a doormat either.

Infuse some beautiful energy into your relationship from afar.

You don't have to say it verbally. Or if you want to want your partner or somebody to react differently, just sit and think of the good things about them in your mind. Try and go there.

Be the bigger person. Be the person who is high vibrational that rises above any situation and sees it for what it is

. That will require courage and some effort, but your efforts will absolutely be rewarded. That reminds me of a time when I had argued with my partner before going to work. I was really annoyed and pissed off and thinking very bad thoughts about him. But you know what? It wasn't going to serve me in any way, it was just making me feel bad.

I decided to disconnect myself from the scenario and tried using empathy, but I didn't have any empathy for him because I couldn't see the situation from his side. So I decided to be the bigger person and energetically pour some love and understanding his way. And it was a different person that walked in through the door that evening.

He reacted to that energetic interaction — which I never told him about — with a positive response and was mindful, which was totally different for him. It was an interesting and productive experiment for me. Try it.

FORGIVENESS LIFE HACK

Forgiveness is one of my life hacks, one of my golden gifts, because when we allow ourselves the freedom of forgiving things from the past it allows us to propel into the future.

Holding a grudge about something you can't forgive will hold you back energetically. It might be that someone has acted against you, you feel betrayed, or you are finding it hard to forgive because what happened goes against your values. There are millions of people in the world and everybody has occasion to forgive every day, whether it's somebody else or especially ourselves.

If you don't forgive, the alternative is living in resentment. That's not manifesting energy, that's not the energy you want to be bringing forward into the future. So your only option is to release yourself from all connection to any past ills or resentments. If you have been wronged in the past, you need to let it go. Not for the other person, nor for any other reason than freeing yourself from the experience so that you can move forward into the future unencumbered by the past.

Things resonate with you when you are awakening and one of the most enlightening things shared with me at one point in my process was that we are forever learning. I learn something new every day, and that makes me feel alive. Nobody in this world knows it all and why would you want to? The idea that learning is where the fun is resonated with me, so I took it on board and I share it when I can.

I was once told that depression resides with people who live in the past. People who live too far forward in the future end up with anxiety and overwhelm because they think too much or too far ahead, while those who stay in the present experience the most joy. You don't have to be a person who makes no plans, and neither do you have to forget the past. There are wonderful experiences in our past, but many of us hold on to the negatives instead of the positives.

Just focus on your beautiful memories. I often flick through my photographs on my phone and it always makes me smile. Photographs are usually of special people and places and happy times in our life, and we often forget about those. That's why photographs are an excellent way to trigger a wonderful emotion and response within you.

Music is also a great reset. When a song comes on it can make you feel good, transcending your energy to a new space, a new sense of being. And that's always wonderful when you need to shift energy. Do anything that makes you feel good.

Forgiveness is one of the most powerful yet hardest of my life principles. We humans find it hard to forgive, especially when we consider somebody has wronged us or when something happens to us that we can't forget, leaving us feeling disgruntled about our life. So, as we have that tendency to hold on to things, we have to start thinking and doing things differently if we want better results. Holding on to the energy of the hurtful experience holds you in the past. That's where negativity hangs out.

When you keep being pulled back to the past, it's energetically draining. Others won't want to be around you because you will deplete their energy. It also doesn't allow you to reach your full potential.

To move forward to a brighter future, you need to let go of the past. But there is a process of freeing yourself. Forgiveness was a big part of the healing for me at a time when my life was changing.

I was catapulted right into Post Traumatic Stress Syndrome because of a fight that took place in my home. It shook me to my core and was a catalyst to me sinking into PTSD for fourteen months. It changed my life and now I can look back with more understanding and forgiveness because yes, the incident was a catalyst for me sinking into PTSD but another scenario at that time could easily have caused the same outcome.

The real issue was that my cup was empty, I had nothing left in my reserves and so I was in a vulnerable space mentally, there was a fine line there. The forgiveness I needed to do was with myself and ensuring that I never let myself down like that again. I fill my cup full and then I can overflow into others.

I need to do some forgiveness around feeling sad for the time I was missing, for how I would react to some scenarios. I'm human!

I was working really hard to maintain a life that I believed was perfect for me and what I wanted at the time. But all my time was consumed with facilitating that life and trying to maintain it. At the time, I didn't understand nor know what other life was sitting there waiting for me to embrace it.

I was knocked right out of my comfort zone and had to face a different reality. After I came through a bit of a dark period, I ended up seeing things brighter and wider, and it was a new beginning. As much as new beginnings can be scary, they are a gift. Change unsettles things, so often people choose to stay with the known. But if we're going to have a better future, we have to do things differently than in the present.

Choosing forgiveness gives us a fresh new start to manifest all of the wonderful things we want in our future.

Anything is possible, and forgiveness is a very big part of that manifesting process. You want to live a magical life? Become courageous. Don't hold on to the past. See through and see past it.

FORGIVENESS AND TIME.

One of the things that I really struggle with is wasting time. Since the pandemic I believe there's been a shift in people's priorities around time. Time has become a more precious commodity than money. We want our lives to return to a state of normality as much as possible, yet there's a feeling of being behind with everything. We're having to prioritise the way we use our time differently because we were forced to, and we don't have the same capacity we had. So that's a transition and transitions are unsettling.

So how do we manage that? How do we transition and shift and gift ourselves time when other people are pushing to do more? Let's put it like this. Those who are constantly adding more activities to their daily schedules are going to experience burnout and that won't serve them well. So you have to use your time in the way that works best for you and the others in your life, and if it isn't working, do something about it.

What we really have to do is forgive ourselves for the time we feel we have wasted. I know I could sometimes do things differently time wise, and I have to shake off any guilt around that, especially around being a mother. I really give myself a hard time when I feel like I've wasted time in other areas that I could have spent with my children instead. Whereas I should honour that, learn from it and not make the same mistake again. While I do that as much as possible, I have to remind myself I am only human and will make mistakes. Besides, these challenges come for a reason. And there's nothing worse than someone coming to the end of their life and not having made the most of their time here.

Time is worth more than any gold. We need to be mindful of

how we use it for it can never be replaced. Are you happy with the way you spend your time? Are you content? Is it working for you? Then wonderful. But if it's not working for you, you have to recalibrate, reprioritise your time and make it work for you. That's how it goes. We need to learn and grow and create space for the magic.

If our lives are totally full of the to-do list, then there's where we're misusing our precious time. We're not leaving room for life, for magic, for the things that can really make a difference in our lives. There has to be room for magic. Even though I talk about this all the time I still have to keep checking in with myself and recalibrating and decluttering. I have to do it intentionally, mindfully and regularly, so the way I spend my time is always evolving.

I invite you to forgive yourself for any time you feel that you've wasted in your life. I invite you to change your perspective about some of the things you've done that could have been done differently, and to understand that sometimes these experiences were necessary for our personal growth, and that's OK. I also want to forgive you and invite you to forgive yourself. Life happens. We do our best.

We do our best with what we have and whatever time we have. So from this moment on, I want you to consider how you prioritise the use of your time. Is it serving you? Could it serve you better? Is there something in your life that you can let go to make room for the magic?

FORGIVING IN THE NOW
WHEN YOU NEED IT

Usually, forgiveness occurs during the healing process after something has happened. But what about those times when you need to shift straight into forgiveness so that you can focus on what needs to be done, instead of falling into shame, grief, sadness or despair. These are all set-back emotions and can consume you when something happens.

I was scheduled to go to the city in Perth for my second TEDx talk filming day at a studio, and one of my kids was sick.

She was thirteen years old, had a high temperature, her colour wasn't good and she was not at all well. But she often got tonsillitis or a virus and was unwell so I sorted her out and went to the city to deliver the TEDx Talk. While I was there, I knew I needed to be home but my friend had driven me so I couldn't just dash back.

When I arrived home she was still unwell. Her sister was with her that day and said that she was really sick.

Little did I know that that evening her body would start to shut down and I would have to rush my unconscious child to the hospital emergency department and then on to the intensive care unit. She ended up being diagnosed with Type 1 Diabetes. We could not have predicted that. It was not on our radar; nobody in our families has it so I wasn't identifying any of the symptoms. All I knew was that she was very unwell. When I had phoned the out of hours doctor that night and was told it would be a few hours before they could come, I knew we couldn't wait so took her straight to emergency.

But by goodness, did I have to shake off the guilt of not identifying that sooner, probably due to my being distracted by doing the TEDx talk. Luckily, she's OK but the outcome could have been different and I have had to shake off the mom guilt.

I had to forgive myself really quickly and say, 'Well, you couldn't have foreseen it.' Yes, I could have been better tuned into my motherly intuition but it wasn't about me and how I felt and the shame I was holding onto. It was about pouring unconditional gold, pure love into her so that I could help her to heal. Instant self-forgiveness was important to allow that to happen.

I've since done other forgiveness work on that scenario, as I held a lot of shame around it because it was a life-or-death situation. I felt it was important to share because others may learn from it.

BEYOND FORGIVENESS

What is beyond forgiveness? The simple answer is, peace.

We all strive for happiness but what we don't realise is that at the core of blissful happiness is peace.

When we have peace in our heart our world is in harmony. And true peace is beyond forgiveness. It is the destination, or as H R Moody describes in *The Five Stages of the Soul,* it is stage five, beyond any stage four breakthrough. It is the destination.

To land at this divine destination we need to tap into greater understanding and empathy that others' actions are emotion fuelled. Please don't think that I am emotionless, if anything I am the opposite, but I choose love first. When someone's actions hurt me, I try to go beyond forgiveness and into empathy and understand the why behind the actions. Often I will have been the receiver of undirected frustration. That does not mean it is OK, quite the contrary as there is always a consequence, but it will be a growth consequence. Let me take you on a journey into alternative thoughts.

Often when we are at the other end of someone else's bad behaviour we feel shame and our instant reaction can be to defend ourselves. When we respond with love, the shame stays with the perpetrator.

I have learned so much about myself by delving into forgiveness to write this book and it's been quite uncomfortable. I always thought I was a forgiving person, but I have since realised that I can forgive, but I don't forget. And then one of the greatest tests of all came, and I actually moved beyond forgiveness.

I recognised that the same issues kept coming up in my

relationship and then it hit me: I wasn't a victim, I had a part to play in reacting, giving precious energy to fuel a fire. It was in this moment that I retracted myself; I found peace in all past interactions and moved beyond the hold they had on me. I forgot in my own way, a way that would allow me to be free of the pain that held me back and facilitated the cycle.

When the same cycle of things kept happening, I chose not to get on that hamster wheel but to forgive and move on. In that space, there is peace, grace, and clarity. And you're not being held back, you're making progress, and that's an important space for us to reach.

Whenever we think of forgiveness, it means that we're raising above whatever it is, because we have done what we can and can do no more.

This is such an empowering, high vibrational energy to go into, and it doesn't dishonour the lessons. The lessons have been learnt and the only thing to do is to be free, move on and be at peace with what's happened. Moving beyond forgiveness and into peace is beautiful. Sometimes you can't resolve things, you can't fix them, you just have to move on and be OK with that.

Especially for those people pleasers in the world who try to tie up all the loose ends. Don't get trapped in the cycle. Move beyond forgiveness, where you free yourself from it. You're in peace, moving on and not holding anything back. It's a special, tranquil destination, one that I am blessed to have experienced.

Peace is possible if you allow yourself to move beyond forgiveness. It's a powerful realisation. It's close to divinity, it enlightens your soul, frees you from darkness and you feel that you're filled with light. It's beautiful. It has been one of the biggest lessons I have had to learn in my lifetime but I'm blessed that I have.

On H R Moody's *Five Stages for the Soul*, this is definitely stage five. It's beyond the struggle, beyond the breakthrough. It's amazing.

I hope that in reading this, it ignites something within you. If not, I hope that it gives you hope and the possibility for peace.

As much as happiness is the destination for many people in life, peace is at the core of that. I'm not talking about materialistic happiness here but divine happiness. And when you move beyond forgiveness, that's where peace truly is. It's just, 'Wow!" and I want you to feel that in your lifetime.

The Beauty
in Belief

You have to believe it to achieve it !

WHAT BELIEFS ARE YOU TELLING YOURSELF?

Be mindful of the stories you're telling yourself, for your subconscious mind will believe them. One of the stories I tell myself is that I love life and it will love me back.

What does that say to you? I love saying that to myself, to my children, to anybody. *Love life and it will love you back.* I talked about it in my TEDx talk called The Forgotten Art of Enjoying Life.

When we show up in loving energy, it super fuels our life because life needs us to show up for it. It doesn't just get lived on its own. It needs us to super fuel it. And when it's super fuelled with love, you will have the best experience.

Why not claim that for yourself? Your thoughts make things happen. Thoughts become things. You can't deny it. So why not choose to have positive thoughts?

Why not choose to think that if you love life, it will love you back? Another of my beliefs that I share is that when time and circumstance align, magic happens. I know this because I've watched it in motion. I've watched it happen. I've experienced it.

There's no better time for something to happen than the right time. Yes, you can have something now, but you may not be ready for it or it may not be ready for you. Why would you want it then? Would you not want it at the best time, when time and circumstance have aligned especially for you?

So be careful what it is that you let your heart believe. Your heart and your mind align together and your beliefs become your reality.

Another of my beliefs is that from every negative situation there is the potential for a positive outcome. I know this because I have had many negative situations in my life as, I'm sure, have you. But it's when I choose to see the positive in the situation, the lesson in it, the opportunity for growth, an evolution in it, that is where I and others around me benefit.

An example of this is when I wrote my first novel. I had a publishing deal and although the publishers were doing their job of publishing my book, I felt no humanity in it. I felt that it was a negative experience because I didn't feel connected to the journey.

That was my perception of the experience. Later, as I became more knowledgeable, I chose to see things differently. I chose to see how much I had learnt during that process and realised I could do some more research, add to my skill set and potentially publish a book myself. And that's what I did. So I took that negative experience of publishing and turned it into a positive.

Little did I know that would be a catalyst to building a publishing empire.

So be mindful of the beliefs that you allow yourself to take on board. You can shift your beliefs, change them any time. That's your choice. Your choice. You are the one who chooses what you believe, not anybody else.

When you're younger, there are belief systems that you take on board from your family, but go ahead and question them if they don't feel aligned with you and your life. Take a moment right now and ask yourself, 'What is a belief that is held by my family that I just don't believe, I don't feel aligned with?' What we believe becomes our experience of life.

If you believe you have to work hard for money, then that's what you will have to do. If you believe, let it be easy, let it flow, the money will come, that's going to be your experience. It's all mind over matter. Investing time in understanding your belief systems and your mindset is an important part of your growth because they affect your experience of life. It's a very important master gift.

The beauty in belief is an important principle that I live by. I choose to see the beauty in it because why take on board other people's beliefs? Why service their beliefs? You need to service your own. You need to honour your own beliefs.

If other people take them on board, then that's fine if they're aligned for them. But nobody should ever impose their belief onto somebody else because a belief should fit like a glove. It shouldn't be a girdle that squeezes us tight and makes us feel restricted. It should be comfortable, feel as if it fits perfectly. So be mindful of the beliefs that you have and if they don't feel aligned, change them.

THE MAGIC IN BELIEF

When others believe in us and when we believe in others, it brings out the magic within someone. Sometimes people don't know their own gifts and we are given the insight into what their gift is. They may not see it for themselves until we voice it or share it. Quite often it comes through a compliment, an observation, or maybe intuitively.

Some things just come to us, we share it with them and it ignites something within them. It may not be in that moment when we say it to them, but our words, our belief, and maybe our actions that follow through for them can spark something in their life that they may not have thought about pursuing. It can be a big catalyst in their life. I speak from experience here, and also from observing other people's success journeys. Quite often, someone will make a comment without any idea it will have a profound impact on the other person's life in that moment.

Think about that. Something you say, such as, 'Goodness, you're a great writer', or 'wow, look at your art', or 'you speak so well and what you've said is so inspiring, you should share your story'—simply appreciating something that somebody else does and seeing value in it. And if it brings them joy and it ignites something within them and they pursue that joy further, well, it's only ever going to bring amazing things into our lives.

Belief, paired with loving intention, makes beautiful things happen in our world, for us and for others, so it has a ripple effect.

It is the best and biggest gift you can give to anyone. Children in particular flourish when they're believed in rather than criticised.

So take a moment to think about what belief is and how it is gifted to others through you, maybe unknowingly. Also take a moment to be aware enough to allow the belief of others in you to reach you. If you have a closed heart, a closed mind, the beauty in belief may never reach you. It may never ignite something within you.

It can feel safe to stay opinionated and not expose your heart to any hurt. Living with an open heart and an open mind takes courage, but that courage is rewarded when you allow these gifts, like the beauty in belief, to reach you when someone else believes in you.

Magic happens in your life and also in theirs. Even if they don't know it, they will feel the benefits, because your gratitude will energetically pour into them. They are tied to that in some way energetically and you supercharging it with your actions allows others to benefit.

So when someone believes in you, and you act on it and love it and have joy in it, it's a good thing for the world, it's not selfish. You're teaching other people to believe in themselves, to back themselves and others, and that it's OK to share what you believe and what you think of others in a positive light. I do not support in any way pulling others down. That makes my heart sore. We're here to rise each other up, and in doing that we are showing others how it's done. It's OK to be positive in others' lives and in our own. In our giving, we receive because people don't forget. The universal laws share with us that what goes around comes around. It may not come from the same source, but it does come back and you can expect it to.

When you give with an open heart with no expectation of return, you get it back tenfold and you deserve it, because in a world that has so much darkness you choose to see the light in it. You choose to be the change that you want to see in this world. You choose to act on something beautiful like the beauty in belief and you make a difference in others' lives and in your own.

Our world needs more of that. It's a truly virtuous gift to do this for yourself and for others.

You see the difference with a child when a teacher comes from a place of belief and encouragement and excitement and enthusiasm for their students' learning and for their gifts. We can't be good at everything, but everybody's good at something. And when you see that something in someone, and encourage and believe in it, you've made magic happen in their life. You have impacted their life profoundly, because there's no going back from that point.

We need more focus on nurturing the gifts within, because if our kids can identify what makes their heart sing at a young age, they will understand that's where to direct their energy. Can you imagine how they will grow and evolve through that?

It's super special. When that level of belief finds you at the best time in the best circumstances, that's when magic happens.

So believing in yourself, believing in others is a loving endeavour, one that requires courage and may come with a backlash. But you've got nothing to lose and everything to gain by believing in others and in yourself.

BELIEF FOR THE NEXT GENERATION.

Have you heard of Dave Fishwick, the self-made UK millionaire whose story is followed in the movie, *The Bank of Dave*? His story is phenomenal and it's so interesting how the Universe lined things up for him.

Dave had a bee in his bonnet about the banks and how they service bonus culture: The banks make money, the fat cats at the top get the big bonuses and the money doesn't go back to the people.

There are very strict legislations around who can open a bank and a bank licence had not been given out globally in 150 years. Even to apply for a licence costs $5 million. Undeterred, Dave put himself in a position where he was able to apply and set up his own bank. His model is a bank system where the money is loaned to people who need it most, even if they would be considered a bit of a risk, because there's trust involved. Any profits that come from returns go back into the community where the bank is situated. It's such a brilliant model.

Dave's belief that anything is possible once you set your mind to it never wavered. He has a business mindset and fundraised the money to establish the bank.

But the big banks brought him to court, saying he had set up his bank illegally. They wanted him sent to prison. So much money was wasted going through the judicial system.

Thank goodness they had a judge who asked, 'What's he here for?' then wanted to know about the bank's model.

Dave's lawyer explained that the money was loaned and any profits were returned to the community so it wasn't for personal gain.

When the judge heard this, he said they were wasting his time bringing Dave to court. How could you send someone to prison for trying to do the right thing? The laws had to change.

Now Dave is trying to change the laws so that all of the money is not being kept to line the pockets of the big guys who happen to work their way up to the top of the food chain. Instead it stays with the people and does good things in the community.

Dave was triumphant, but can you imagine? Just put yourself in his place. Here he is, a businessman who owns a mini bus company, and he's been lucky and made a lot of money from it, but he also has a goodwill legacy mindset. He knows he has to make a difference.

His model will change the financial structure of the whole world and make it a better place. He really believes in it, yet here they are bringing him to court because of something he's trying to do for the good of others, he's being blamed for doing wrong. Ethically, that's wrong.

I'm sure what happened took a lot out of him and his family. And I'm sure he must have had some doubts about what he was doing at times. But he didn't let that deter him from his passion for what he wanted to achieve in life and for others. Belief in the path is the fuel that keeps you going, even when big companies block your way forward.

Dave wanted to right what he believed was wrong and stood firm on that. It's a beautiful example of somebody who's really standing for what they believe in and making a big difference for the masses, because not everybody would have the strength and courage that he has had to do this.

Hollywood came knocking on his door because of what happened and I recommend you watch the movie. I recently listened to an interview with him on Nova Radio here in Australia, and this man really impressed me. He's not doing this for personal gain. He's doing it because he believes that this will make a change. And by goodness, do we not need more people standing for what they believe in, for humanity?

This has impact. This is the little guy saying to the big guys, no, I'm not going away. You are doing wrong and you're not bullying me out of it.

His story influenced me. It showed me that I have to stand up for what I believe in because it will ripple and have a positive effect for someone else, shining a light for them.

BORROWING OTHERS' BELIEF UNTIL YOURS KICKS IN

Belief can be instilled in us in many different ways. Your perspective of belief is also important. For me the beauty in belief is when we don't believe in ourselves, and we allow others to see the beauty within us and we adopt our beauty from them and adapt it to our lives. The most gorgeous things come out of that. Our belief systems that we inherit through our childhood and through our families often don't serve us into adulthood. Often we have to unlearn a lot of things and then really find ourselves, and that takes effort.

It also takes awareness, acceptance, and forgiveness. We have to forgive, because much of what we inherit is passed on unintentionally. We just have to move on from that and become the best version of ourselves in the future. If our families didn't do that for themselves, then that's their burden to bear. But you are responsible for becoming your best version so stop distracting yourself with the past, forgive and move on.

When we don't have self-belief but then somebody sees something in us that we don't see in ourselves, it conjures something up within us that is a truly magical gift. If you're mindfully aware and are noticing other signs and affirmations all around you, it is letting you know this is a calling, this is on your path to your best self.

I can identify it on my own journey. I never would have believed it possible to write 50,000 words in a month had it not been for a conversation with a friend during a picnic at a play park. She told me she wrote for a few hours every Thursday and had already written 50,000 words of her personal story. She never planned to publish it but was finding it therapeutic on her healing journey.

Wow, that's powerful, I thought.

As a result of this conversation, when I discovered NaNoWriMo which challenges writers to produce 50,000 words of a novel during November, my limiting belief had been replaced with possibility. The prospect of writing that many words was no longer daunting. I had recently experienced an epiphany and subsequently had a calling to write my own story. Everything was aligned — my belief that it was possible, my call to action, and the opportunity to write and release the pent-up sadness and grief of losing my twins.

This call was very loud, so I honoured it and wrote my first book, *The Visitor*. Doing that was a huge catalyst in my life.

But had I not been introduced to the idea that it was possible, I would never have taken the next step. By sharing our stories, we show others what's possible. Then they have the belief in themselves when it's time for them to show up to do things in their life.

When someone lacks self-belief and you give them your perspective on what you see in them, you're helping them see themselves through a different lens. That is a truly valuable gift. They may be resistant to it, but the actual calling for you to share with them your perspective of what you see in them won't go to waste, it will be absorbed. And when the time comes, they will take the necessary action. I am often told, 'When you said that to me, I didn't believe it at first, but then something happened and I remembered it and believed it.'

Gifting people these different perspectives of themselves so that they can see themselves in a different light is such a beautiful thing. It can allow magic to happen for them and for others around them. Everyone benefits. So never take for granted the beauty of gifting belief to someone else or to yourself, because all goodness comes from that source.

It is a love fuelled thing to do.

BELIEF AND SELF-TALK

Believe with all of your being that what you want in your life is coming to you. Put it out there and believe with all your heart that it's on its way. Act as if you already have it.

There's so much energy and passion in that, whether it's to do with money, relationships, an experience. Whatever it is, you believe it with all of your heart and act as if you have it. You have the courage to act on inspired thoughts and have no fear around it.

When you do that, wonderful things happen in your life. You shift the energy and are grateful for what you have. You are grateful for the passion you have in your heart. You become grateful for everything, and you see the difference almost immediately with the potential of what can happen in your life. It's really something special. It's something to really hold on to because that's where the magic is in life.

I could talk about life magic all the time, because you have to see something first in your mind to have it in your hand. Every single thing on this planet started with a thought, because thoughts are energy. Everything starts and ends with energy. It's hard to fathom, isn't it? But at the core of every atom is energy. What do you think energises it to grow, to multiply, to mould into something amazing.

Really delve into that thought and allow yourself to sit with it.

Activate it by writing it down. What it is that you want out of life? What do you want to experience? What is it? Just believe with all of your heart that it is coming. Activate it.

THE BEAUTY OF BELIEF
IN MOTHERHOOD

This is an important one to talk about because when we become parents, our identity shifts. Women especially go through a lot physically and emotionally in giving birth. In motherhood, we lose a little bit of ourself, but also find a lot of ourselves.

Many mums take time off from the workforce to be present with their child. This can be six weeks, six months, or six years. Some choose to be fully present as a mum until their children are grown and independent, perhaps even parents themselves.

Mum mode is such a contrast to work mode. There's no downtime, especially in the early years. Mothering is constant. When you're getting back into finding out who you are and what it is you want to do after taking that motherhood break, belief in yourself can be shaky. You are likely older and things have changed.

Motherhood means being an emotional mess sometimes, but in that space we find the love, the core, the source. When we connect with that love, core and source, that's when we can find the magic of life if we don't overthink it. Embrace it, enjoy it. Find your new normal that you absolutely adore for you and your family, so that you're not feeling like you are compromising any of yourself, but are still able to pursue your ambitions and dreams.

That requires belief in yourself and your ability. Sometimes we have to lean on others and borrow what they say of us so that we can start believing in ourselves again. I know that was certainly the case for me when I had my second child. Not so much with my first because I was kind of a lone parent, and while my son's dad was around it was very much me who made the decisions.

When I had my second child it was a totally different scenario. I was breastfeeding and all the emotions and self-doubt came in, so it was hard. But sometimes our biggest breakthroughs come through adversity. We had just emigrated to Australia when I had my third child and being at home with my kids gifted me precious time to discover my dreams and begin the journey of exploration towards my true calling. When I started to find my new me, I discovered that I had brain space. I allowed myself this creativity to explore new things and it was beautiful.

We started doing children's books around our kitchen table. We made it an activity and as I was exploring new things the kids were enjoying themselves. This was beautiful and just lit me up. Then I had my fourth child and I was called loudly towards writing my first novel, *The Visitor*, which was a creative process and one that I just purged out of me in 30 days during a NaNoWriMo challenge. That didn't mean I wasn't present for my kids. I had a four-week-old baby at the time, so when I was breastfeeding, I was typing my book. It just worked, and it filled my cup and helped me be a better mum.

Even though things change and transition with motherhood and there are ebbs and flows and sometimes you feel like you're the worst mother in the world, believe in yourself. You need to be able to tap into your inner belief in yourself and the belief that anything's possible. Whenever your heart and mind are aligned with it, you can make anything happen. You will be gifted the strength, the knowledge, and the way.

So it's time to start enjoying yourself and believing in yourself, because if I can do it as a mum of six, you can too. You can find your dream life, and it won't be the same as mine. That would probably be a lot of people's worst nightmare but for me it's my dream life. It's busy, it's fast, it's furious. There are also days where it's slow and messy and loving and caring and movies and chocolates and beach walks. So I have it all and I'm blessed. Today I'm on my way to the city where I have a lunch organised. So mum's dreaming, mum's doing, mum's actioning. But mum will be home in a few hours and she'll be back, showing up for herself and nurturing her kids.

A family belief exercise.

Give everyone a pen and paper.

Allow 10 seconds for each answer.

Allow this to be anonymous and allow members of the family to destroy their responses if they want to.

- What do you believe with all your heart?
- What is the thing you want to achieve most in life?
- What is stopping you from achieving it?
- Do you believe that you can have ANYTHING you want in life?
- What is so precious to you that you would not like to give up?
- Is there a belief in our family that you don't agree with? If so, what is it and what do you believe instead?

Afterwards, read each question individually and ask if anyone wants to share their answer.

For those who don't share remind them that they know themselves a little better now and to be mindful of the belief story they are telling themselves.

Repeat this annually.

LIMITLESS BELIEFS

I want to share with you a little master class that I do when I work with people who haven't awakened to their potential. The reason I am so passionate about helping people awaken to their full potential is because anything is possible. There is nothing that you can't achieve whenever you set your mind to it. If you want it, you can have it.

You can make all the excuses in the world not to achieve something, but the fact is, if you want it, you can achieve it. All it takes is for you to set an intention, take inspired action and follow through. You must have the courage to follow through. Invest in yourself, whether that be time or money. Connect with the right people and feel very in tune with what it is that you want to achieve.

You can achieve anything you want to achieve in your life when you believe it possible. At the age of 46 I have achieved more than many people do in ten lifetimes. And why is that? It's because I don't have any limits to what I believe. I know that anything is possible when I set my mind to it.

I have the courage to pursue all my dreams and desires and the courage to action whatever needs to be actioned. I'm also very strategic. I'm connected to my ability to know what is the next step on my journey to receiving what I want to attract. One of the things that I always bring it back down to is self- awareness, because we need to do the work on ourselves to become aware of our abilities, where our strengths lie and what we are capable of achieving at any one time. We need to increase that awareness when we want to achieve big things.

The big thing is getting clear on what it is that you really want.

Many people do not actually know that. They get too confused, they want too many things; or they think they want something, when actually they don't because it's not aligned with their higher purpose. I need you to take a moment to identify what it is that's aligned with your values, because you do not want to compromise any of yourself in the process of receiving. This is a huge mistake.

I see many people do this when they are manifesting or achieving things that they believe are impossible. So know your values, know what matters to you, because honestly, you don't want to sacrifice any of this on the journey if you go for something you want and achieve it. I love being a mum of six, but I also love achieving things. I don't have any limitless beliefs, so I can make anything happen.

But what if something I want to happen compromises my values? Is it worth it? For me, that is a 'Hell, no'. So when I am setting intentions and pursuing goals, I always make sure that I truly understand what it's going to take to make something happen.

Is it aligned with my values and is it worth it? Because I can guarantee you, by the time you get to the destination of receiving that goal, if you must compromise your values, it will not be worth it. No monetary or personal goal is worth compromising your values, whether that be family or part of yourself. You've got to really understand, 'What is it going to take from me for this to happen?'

If you're able to do that, to really identify what it is that you want, then what you can make happen is aligned with your values, and also the good you can do for others through your journey. It's always good to give. There are amazing cultures in the world that give ten per cent of all their earnings to a charity. They know that by giving part of what they receive to others, more keeps coming; gratitude is poured into them.

If you cannot see too far ahead or if things feel overwhelming when you think of limitless beliefs, then take it step by step. Set the goal but then just go on the journey and take one step at a time until you get there. I set the intention of building a million-dollar publishing press. I thought it would take me 25 years but I dedicated myself to the journey and remained open and in tune with my knowing and it only took me seven years.

And so how do you do that? You're just open, you're aware and you have the courage to take action when need be.

Think about it.

Understand that certain intentions, inspired thoughts, and opportunities are going to come in unconventional ways because you can't change anything if you keep doing everything in the same way. The same actions get the same results, so in order to achieve different things you've got to think differently. You've got to action different things and have the courage to do that. That of course is outside of our comfort zones.

But I can tell you one hundred per cent that the magic happens just one step outside of our comfort zones. And if you have the courage to step outside of that comfort zone every time you take an action, guess what you're going to be doing? You're going to be reaching limits that never seemed possible before. You're going to surpass any ceiling that you ever had.

Do you know how that feels when you get there? When you know that's not the end of it, that you have more to come? That whenever you set a goal or intention, you have surpassed it tenfold? Sometimes when we set the intention to achieve something, where we're at right then in our mind makes it hard for us to see further, because it's beyond us.

But when we believe in ourselves without setting limits, we can make the most amazing things happen. There's no ceiling on what we can achieve. It's only what we believe in our minds.

Believing in ourselves is one of the biggest and most important things that we can gift ourselves. If you don't believe in yourself in the first instance, lean on someone who believes in you and be energised by that. Take action from that, because believe me, whenever people believe in you, it's very motivating.

If I hadn't been believed in when I started out in my journey, I wouldn't be where I am today. It's because someone believed in me and my work that I started to believe in myself.

If no one's believing in you, then you're not in the right circle. You've got to surround yourself with people who rise you up. And each one of those people who rise you up is a believer.

So think limitlessly. Leave room for the magic and don't be afraid to share the journey, both the triumphs and the tribulations. We need more people sharing their triumphs. It is wonderful that so many people are sharing their vulnerabilities, but the success stories also shouldn't be kept to ourselves.

That's not the way the world is supposed to work. We're supposed to learn how to do something and share those skills with other people. I often get asked, 'Karen, how do you do it?' because it seems totally illogical for a mother of six to achieve everything that I've achieved. Yet I don't overthink it.

I will someday sit and write my life story from A to B about how I got there. Right now, I'm forward focused. I don't reside in the past, I supercharge the present. That ensures my future is always bright. And it's only because I have the courage and the foresight and the belief that anything is possible should I choose to achieve it.

But I always, always make sure that whatever I set my intentions on achieving is aligned with my values. Otherwise, it's not worth it.

ONE BELIEF AWAY

You are one belief away from making your dreams come true. For me, there's a saying that I resonate with and it may help you: We can't control everything, but we can control some things.

If you can't change something, change the way you think about it. Perspective is everything when it comes to beliefs.

When something's not working for you, look at what you are accepting as your reality. If it no longer serves you, challenge that belief. Find something that works better for you and experience the shift that takes place around you. It's only a small adjustment, but so important, because if you're not getting the results you want in life, you need to make changes. The only way you're going to get different results is if you do things differently.

It doesn't have to be drastic. I do say that magic happens just outside of your comfort zone, but that doesn't mean you have to take a running leap and land so far from your comfort zone that you get overwhelmed and feel totally uncomfortable.

You don't need to alter your beliefs in such a shocking way that it goes against every grain of your being and becomes a big culture shock. In saying that, you do need to make some adjustments and recalibrate yourself. Usually whenever life throws you a curveball, it's not to dislodge you or knock the stuffing out of you. It's actually a gift, an opportunity for you to recalibrate. You're either stuck or you're not feeling courageous enough to pursue something. Going around on the same merry go round may be fun at the beginning, but it's not going to serve you in your life progression.

We're all in cycles of life, but we're not all in the same cycle. Individually we shift through different cycles all the time.

Numerology talks about life cycles defining your life transitions from one phase to the next, and while I resonate with that thinking, I see cycles differently.

I believe we are called to something, and we pursue it. We're curious, we're nervous, we're learning new things and it's wonderful yet also scary. With that curious thought, we've planted a seed and it's up to us whether we're going to nourish it and allow it to grow, but as soon as it starts sprouting, we go on a cycle with it.

There are different cycles in my life when things happen faster because I'm in more in flow, I may have had a creativity spike. I planted more seeds in a different cycle. There are so many different ways it can come to be and you simply have to embrace that, without overthinking. Just go with the flow. And that is not somebody else's flow or somebody else's perception of what your flow should be. It is your flow. You will know you are in flow by the feeling within you and the ease of getting results on the outside.

Things happen and you can consciously keep yourself in flow as much as possible. But life is life. We're spiritual beings that are constantly growing, and in order to grow in spirit, we must endure challenges. Challenges are not a bad thing.

A lot of people's belief systems around challenges in life are that they are a roadblock. Challenges are not a roadblock. A challenge is an opportunity for you to do the work so that you grow into the next version of yourself.

It's a stepping stone towards your calling, your dreams, your purpose, whatever you want to call it. If you do the work and learn from the challenges, you will break through the struggle. You will have a breakthrough where you will happy dance because everything will just fall into place and you will be rewarded. And that, my friend, is the most beautiful, divine, high vibrational experience you will have in life. I'm sure you will have had these experiences in your life, but you may not have been aware of them. So be mindfully aware that if you are having a challenge, it is what you need to take the next step towards your dreams, and you'll do the work because it's worth it. Inner work is the most important work.

Another belief system that serves me well is that way too many people lean outside themselves for the answers. Yet those answers being loudly shouted by others may not be the answers for you. So don't take them as your answers unless they deeply connect with your soul. Your soul is a navigation tool for you. Whenever it ignites, stirs something within you, that's a call to action.

If you feel nothing, it's not for you, it's a 'Hell, no'. But when it ignites something within you, it's a 'Hell, yes'. And by God, have the courage to take the next step. It will always require courage, but it doesn't require too much intelligence because everything you need, the navigation system, is within you. All the answers are within you.

You know them. Don't overthink it. Intuitively move forward in the pursuit of your dreams, of your purpose, of the highest version of yourself.

I promise you that if you follow this, you will live a life so much higher than anyone else can ever guide you on because you're internally driven. So lean inwards for the answers and outwards for the support to make it happen. Can you do that for yourself? Can you give it a try?

These are formulas to help you connect to your core belief and also help you mould your own belief systems that serve you. The belief systems that you have in place will serve you and you alone. They won't serve your children, or your partner, they won't serve a stranger or a mentee. But you can share your thoughts and your story for others to benefit and get inspired.

If you promise someone results and you're not guiding them to do the work, then they're in trouble and so are you. The important thing about self-development is that the journey is where the learning and the growth take place. You cannot bypass the journey.

You can't pay somebody else to grow for you.

That's an inner job. Nobody can go inside your soul and do the work for you. You must endure and you can get support. The smart and most efficient way is to identify exactly what it is that you want and need and then lean outwards for the support to make it happen. You can call in a mastermind, you don't have to learn all the skills, but you do have to identify the need and then put in place and delegate what it is that you want to achieve. It's the only way. You can't avoid it.

Why would you want to avoid it? When you do the work, you experience and discover new things. Why would you want somebody else to do that for you? They will never be as connected to your journey as you are.

Believe me, if you are not enjoying the journey, you are not on the right journey.

So many people set goals and want to get the results, to reach the top of the mountain without having to walk. Well then, why bother? You just want the view. You don't want the journey. The journey is where all the learning is and when you get to that summit, you go, 'Hell yes, I earned this and I'm going to enjoy every moment of it.'

Then you will choose another journey and embark on that.

That's life. There's no way in the world you should ever gift that over to somebody else and nobody else will ever do it to the highest capacity that you can. So don't try to bypass your journey. You will be the one that suffers in the long term.

Life is for living and for loving and it loves you back when you live it.

Think happy thoughts and they'll come back to you. Think happy thoughts and the whole world seems brand new. So hijack some gratitude to change the vibe. Shift your beliefs ever so slightly and see your world change in the most beautiful, magnificent way.

THE MOST IMPORTANT STORY
YOU WILL EVER TELL YOURSELF

Belief is one of the important master gifts because how we develop our belief system plays a big part in our future experience. The good news is that we can recalibrate our belief system if it isn't working for our greatest good. We do have to set the intention and do the work that will feel a little out of our natural comfort zone for a while, but our efforts are always rewarded when we act on inspired thoughts.

I could never have become a writer if I did not challenge my self-belief about my worthiness. I believed that writers were other very smart people, and I couldn't possibly be one, but I soon discovered that my words are valuable.

Become so mindful of the story you tell yourself that you are super vigilant with only harvesting productive thoughts. The type of thoughts that help you harvest the next chapter of your life. Ask yourself what it is that you want out of the next month, year, five years, ten years— and start acting as if you have it. It is in our emotion fuelled actions and beliefs that we manifest the next step for ourselves, so we need to show up with enthusiasm and confidence, with unwavering belief that our next chapter feels as if it is already written in the stars, we just need to claim it. This is a beautiful melody of life and when we stick to that rhythm we will feel as if magic is all around us and that we are living at a higher vibration. Our thoughts and actions will be rewarded because we have the courage to have faith, call it in and action it.

So be super vigilant about what you expose yourself to, take action towards your dreams daily and keep your peripheral vision on because the opportunities and inspired thoughts will come from left of centre and you will have to be ready to action them.

Magic truly happens when you believe.

A belief exercise:

Every day take three impulsive actions towards activating your intention.

(The key is to not preplan. Instead, allow yourself to be inspired every day)

BELIEF AND ENERGY

At the core of everything is energy, energy we can influence with our thoughts. Energy is fuel for us, so we need to understand how important it is and nurture it, gift it the time and the space in our lives to be mindful of it.

When I embraced this way of thinking about energy and about us as humans on this Earth, it changed how I saw, interacted and experienced things. It's all about energy. Look at the diagram below, and study it for a moment.

Our belief systems need to incorporate the scientific knowledge around energy. This visualisation really changed how I perceived energy.

We are all energy fields. A tree is energy. A butterfly is energy. Everything is energy because it's created from the source; God is energy. Everything is energy. It's just always coming through in different forms.

Energy is not static. It's always recycling, rejuvenating, reinventing. I think that's why I love innovation so much. Something new is being born. Whether it's a thought or something that's going to be made, it's energy. This universe is the biggest thing we know and energy is at the core of everything that is!

When it comes to our bodies, we're all comprised of atoms, and at the core of every atom is energy, so it all starts and ends with energy. I never gave it much thought until I really took a moment and understood how fundamental energy is in the creation of all things. Even in the creation of a materialistic object, in the creation of the thoughts that gifted the inventors the knowledge to create what they did, everything is energy. When I'm driving, I look around me and think, *Wow! Look at this big truck here. It's made of energy. It's an energy field, it's an energy source. It's made with material things, but it's energy.*

The universal flow of energy:

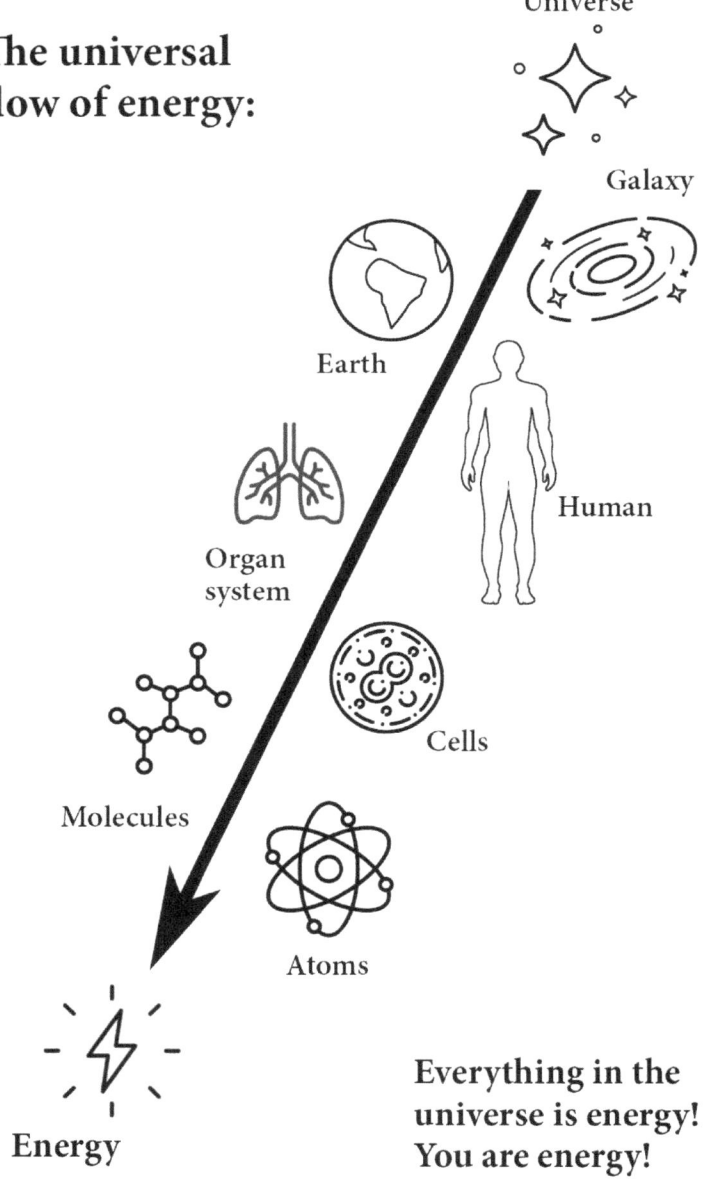

Everything in the universe is energy! You are energy!

That to me shows the power that is energy. Take a moment to think about that. Use your energy for one moment to pause and understand why it's important for you to protect your energy because it absolutely alters your experience of life, it changes the reality within you and surrounding you.

Check in with yourself and not just this once. Check in every now and again to make sure you are keeping your energy on track. It's a continuous job but as with anything, you have to shift your mindset. I always talk about creating a 21-day habit to establish a new routine. If you prioritise your energy, get enough sleep, get rid of toxicity around you and do this mindfully for 21 days, your health will benefit.

Remember, at the centre of you, of every atom in your body that creates every single healthy and unhealthy experience, there's energy. Our energetic experiences have a profound effect on us emotionally and physically so when we take care of our energy, we're healthier and may avoid various illnesses and afflictions.

My husband had really upset me on one of my birthdays and I had to go into work. I was emitting such a powerful energy of sadness and hurt that a colleague felt it from two aisles away. She gravitated to me and said, 'Karen, are you OK, because I'm feeling really something off today with you. I can't get you out of my head.'

Of course she could sense it because I could feel it pulsating from me. Now that is not a healthy energy. That is not an energy that was going to nourish my body.

Luckily our bodies are our human DNA. Our biology is so powerful. Our bodies regenerate all the time, they heal. It's an absolute miracle what happens in our bodies every day. We can help them. Our health is our wealth. You can have all the money in your world but if you don't have health, you don't have wealth in my eyes.

We need to take care of our health and the health of our loved ones. It's fundamental to our experience of life, so take care of your energy. Your energy is what feeds everything within you and around you. Really believe in that and take a moment to nurture that for yourself and for others around you.

It's not rocket science. You don't need to have a PhD to understand that energy is important. You do need to have strong intentions and want to really nurture your energy. It takes a moment.

Humanity needs us all to focus on our energy. Let's do it. Let's make a difference in our world so that we can have a ripple effect and make a difference in others, and then in the greater picture, the grander picture.

LIFE MAGIC AND BELIEF

"Magic" can be seen as a metaphorical representation of a profound sense of connection, inspiration, and alignment with one's true self and purpose. It is the feeling of being in flow, where synchronicities occur, opportunities arise, and everything seems to fall into place. This sense of magic can be a powerful indicator that we are on the right path and aligned with our deepest desires and aspirations.

Belief in this "life magic" involves having trust and courage in following our intuition and inner guidance. It requires us to listen to that inner voice, to embrace uncertainty, and to take inspired action despite any fears or doubts we may have. Believing in life magic means recognising that there is a greater force at work, a universal intelligence or interconnectedness that guides us when we are open to it.

By cultivating belief in life magic, we open ourselves to the possibility of extraordinary experiences, opportunities, and synchronicities that can lead to personal growth and fulfilment. It encourages us to see the world with wonder and curiosity, to embrace the unknown, and to be receptive to the unexpected and seemingly miraculous.

However, it is important to note that belief in life magic does not imply a disregard for practicality or a reliance solely on external forces. It is about finding a balance between intuition and action, between surrender and personal responsibility. It's about recognising that our beliefs, thoughts, and actions shape our reality and that by aligning ourselves with our inner magic, we can create the life we desire.

Ultimately, whether one believes in life magic is a personal perspective. Some may find comfort and inspiration in the concept, while others may approach life from different frameworks. What matters most is finding a belief system that resonates with one's own values, aspirations, and understanding of the world, supporting personal growth, and living a fulfilling life.

BELIEF AND VISUALISATION

I want to share with you a quick story about the power of visualisation, the choices you make and the beliefs that you hold.

In 2020, I set the intention that I wanted to do a TEDx talk. Now when I set an intention, I always fuel it with love, put it out there into the universe, and then take action on inspired thoughts. Even when I don't have foresight into what may result, I just know that I have to do it. One day I happened to be on a call that had no relation to TEDx. Then the next day I got a message saying, 'I have to have you on my TEDx stage.'

I was invited by simply being me. I said yes, of course, and got excited. Then COVID hit and I wasn't going to be able to be on the TEDx stage because I had to be there in person. It was on the other side of the world from where I live so I had to reluctantly tell the organiser that I could not attend as a speaker and my spot would have to be given to someone else. This broke my heart and I could have sunk into self-pity.

For some reason, though, I went out onto my patio and stood there feeling immense gratitude, peace, and love, especially for my family. I also felt proud of myself for not compromising my values for ambition. That's one of the things I really identified with, so I asked myself the question: What would be three things that would be perfect for you to have your TEDx talk?

I wanted to do a TEDx women's event because I had just won a Women Will Change the World award. I wanted to speak on a stage in Perth so that I didn't get stranded somewhere in the world unable to get back to my children, or if they came with me, that we didn't all get stuck away from home. And three, I wanted to do it in 2020, not 2021, when the other TEDx was scheduled. Bear in mind that this was September and there wasn't much left of 2020. There were no fish biting and there were no prospects. This was what came to my mind.

So I simply sat in that feeling of it happening, being wonderful, and ticking that box that year, because I offset a powerful intention every year. Then I left it, and went and picked up my kids from school. The very next day, I got a phone call saying, 'Hey, Karen, TEDx got on to me last night. They want me to host a TEDx Women event. It's a virtual event, so that means you can do it on a stage in Perth. There are three things you have to do. It's going to be TEDx Women, it's going to be on a stage in Perth and it's going to be in six weeks' time. Can you do it?'

This nearly blew my mind. I hadn't shared what I had visualised with anybody and the very next day I was being asked the three things that were my sacred requests to the universe. In that moment, I knew the power of visualisation. What went on to blow my mind even more was that it happened three times and I ended up doing a TEDx talk in 2020, 2021 and 2022. I adored the one in 2022. It wasn't a Signature Talk, but it was a talk on my sister's stage in front of an audience. It was called The Forgotten Art of Enjoying Life and I was so relaxed, so happy.

I knew the first two lines of what I was going to say and the rest just flowed. This tied up my TEDx experience beautifully, because I believe in the magic of three and how things come full circle in threes. It seems to be a theme in my life that when I set a powerful intention for one, I seem to get three. The same happened when I set the intention in 2022 to win a Stevie Award for Women in Business and I won gold, silver and bronze. There's no way in the world I could have predicted that.

MANIFESTING FORMULA

I'm going to share with you a quick story about how I became a Law of Attraction practitioner. I watched the spiritual documentary *The Secret* and also *You Can Heal Your Life* by Louise Hay and I've mentioned in previous books that they gave me a foundation to awaken.

I had already been going through a kind of spiritual awakening, writing down my musings and unconsciously discovering things myself. Then I started to become more conscious and aware.

The idea of having the power of thoughts frightens some people whereas for me it was as if someone gifted me the biggest golden wand ever. I was so ecstatic that I could have control over my thoughts and it really empowered me, so I wanted to play around with it and see what I could make happen. I felt connected to Joe Vitali, who features in *The Secret*, so I followed up and saw that he was running a Law of Attraction course.

I enrolled, completed the course and passed the test. Then I was invited to study to become an advanced Law of Attraction practitioner to teach other people. The course was a bit more intense than the first one, but I loved it and I loved getting to know things. Once I had completed the course, passed the test and received my certification, I never told anyone but thought, 'I'm going to really play with this and see what I can make happen.' I'd already written my first novel and I was starting to publish books at this time.

I decided to set a big fat audacious goal. And my big fat audacious goal was to build a million-dollar publishing press. Now, I did not know how this was going to come about. My studies were in humanities, not in publishing; but I knew I had a passion for story and such a faith and trust in the journey, because it's my job to set the intention and then it is the universe's job to bring it in.

I have to act on inspired thoughts and opportunities that are aligned with that goal. So I set myself a goal of investing $50 a week into this venture, thinking, 'Let's see where it goes.' Any money I made, I reinvested and I got I koala ? deal, I had some people publish their books with me and lots of things happened.

I'd put the money into the business, done the work and people got services from me for free, but it was building up the press. You give, you receive, and I have received a millionfold since then. So I went on the journey and it was really interesting. I had thought it would take me twenty-five years to build a million-dollar press but no, in the seventh year I had a million dollar year. Yeah, I spent a million dollars, because my whole model was to reinvest as I was going along. So I was head down, bum up, making things happen and reinvesting to make bigger things happen.

To this day we're still doing that, but right now we have set a newer goal, which is amazing and phenomenal. Instead of a million-dollar press we are heading for a ten-million-dollar press and I can't wait for you to see that happen for us. If there's something I want to experience or achieve, I set a powerful intention. I really connect with my power of knowing and if it's a 'hell, yes!' for it, I give it my all.

And yes, life happens. Yes, there are challenges, because challenges may help us grow into the version of ourselves that we need to be for that goal to happen.

But there's never one moment that I waver from the belief that I'm on the path, because I'm saying 'hell, yes!' to the things I know are aligned with them, even if it seems irrational. In my life, the irrational actions I have taken are always connected with my knowing and once I have the courage and faith to step into them, I always reap the rewards. They are a super fuel to the success that I have had and experienced. I get tested. A lot.

But my faith is unwavering, and I know and I desire and so I continue. Right now, I'm on a big cycle, and before any breakthrough, there's always a struggle. The struggle is real, but so are the breakthroughs. It's important not to abandon things in the struggle, because the struggle just means something's imminent. My advice for you when you're in a struggle is to feed your mind, nurture your mind with growth thoughts, read books, listen to audiobooks, distract yourself with something productive that lights and fills you up.

Keep your energy going but honour the unsteady feeling, honour the change, honour the growth and do the work and you will be rewarded beyond your wildest dreams. My hopes and dreams have been realised tenfold. We signed the Duchess of York to the press; we've had amazing things happen and my cup is full. Please know it is when we just get on with the doing of life and make amazing things happen that it all flows together.

If you don't believe in the power of the law of attraction, then you will not achieve what it is you want. You'll just think it's a farce. But when you've achieved it, and you are aware and mindful of how it's come about, you're going to live your best life and you're going to be able to redo that, relive it every time with whatever intention you set. Enjoy every moment of the process, for joy is at the essence of all success!

*The world is full of magic,
waiting for us to learn
how to use it.*

W.B YEATS

CONCLUSION

Well, did that ignite anything within you? I share my master gifts in a flow that works for me. They may jiggle around a bit, you know; sometimes intention comes before knowing, and love is at the core of all my master gifts. But you may have to go with belief first or forgiveness or whatever you need to lead with. Just embrace.

There's no wrong way to embrace these gifts. You've just got to go with what resonates and what calls to you at any given time. Honor your journey, and you will be rewarded. That's how it goes. You will be called back to this book many times because as you grow, as you pivot, as different gifts are required at different points in your life, you will be called back to harness what's channelled through me, right into your heart and mind, so that you can advance feeling supported and cared for.

And everything I do is with loving intention. So, I hope that you feel that. I hope that you've enjoyed journeying with me in this book, and I hope that I journey with you for a lifetime. So come and join me. You can check me out on socials or come and join my website.

There's lots of free content on there, or you can visit my YouTube channel. I look forward to being a positive presence in your life, and please reach out and share anything you need with me.

*When time and
circumstance align,
magic happens.*

ABOUT K.P. WEAVER

K.P. Weaver is a visionary author, accomplished publisher, and life philosopher known for her profound insights into mindfulness, knowing, intention, love, gratitude, forgiveness, and belief. With a remarkable career spanning various genres, including novels, motivational literature, children's books, and journals, she has consistently led the way in her authorship, generously sharing her transformative philosophies through the power of the written word.

Her journey is a testament to the boundless potential of human existence. As an award-winning author and a TEDx Speaker, she has not only penned numerous books but also touched the hearts and minds of readers worldwide. Her work transcends traditional literary boundaries, offering profound wisdom and guidance in diverse facets of life.

In addition to her prolific writing career, Karen has emerged as a prominent figure in the publishing world. Having built a highly successful publishing empire from the ground up, she has nurtured major authors, authored over 40 impactful books, and established her own credible brand in the market. Her innovative strategies and techniques are anchored in the power of "Knowing" to manifest dreams and aspirations into reality.

A recognized, gifted teacher who inspires others to harness the magic of life. She imparts her transformative wisdom through her 7 life principles, each a masterful element in her journey to success. These principles serve as a guiding light, illuminating the path to personal growth, fulfillment, and achievement. Her biggest call to action was to awaken those who sleep through the power of story.

Her life philosophy revolves around the idea that when

mindfulness, intention, love, gratitude, forgiveness, and belief converge at the right time and circumstance, true magic happens. Her life and work stand as a testament to the boundless potential that resides within each of us.

To find out more visit her website www.kpwofficial.com or follow her on all social media platforms.

Milton Keynes UK
Ingram Content Group UK Ltd.
UKHW020422270324
439757UK00012B/85